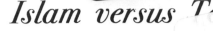
Islam versus Terrorism

An Intimate

Understanding Islam and the
Culture of the Middle East

Firooz Eftekhar Zadeh

Library of Congress Control Number: 2002093852

DS 35.62 .Z33 2002
Zadeh, Firooz Eftekhar, 1938
-
Islam versus terrorism

Twin Lakes Publishing Inc.
www.vtinet.com/swiss

Cover by: Pearson Design, Evergreen, CO.

Photo: Prophet's Mosque, Medina - Courtesy of:
Alavi Foundation, 500 Fifth Ave. New York, NY. 10110

Dedication

This book is dedicated to all victims of terror in the world, their families and loved ones with hopes and prayers that with understanding and compassion we may be able to change terrorism to love and harmonious living.

Acknowledgments

I would like to thank Masood Ahmad, my good friend, for his perspective and viewpoint sent from Pakistan; Ashleigh Banfield and Brian Williams of MSNBC, for their insightful, straightforward reporting; Ted Koppel of NightLine, Barbara Walters and the staff of ABC for their outstanding coverage of the Middle East, Fox News reporters, and CBS 60 Minutes, Yahoo Internet World Factbook; the Organization of Islamic Conference, and all the authors, whose books I had the privilege of reading and occasionally quoting.

Special thanks to Cheryl Fluehr, the entertainment manager of Holland America Cruise Lines, and their outstanding staff for giving me the opportunity to share my ideas with others. And of course a sincere thanks to the wonderful passengers for encouraging me to write my lectures in the form of this book.

I would most particularly like to thank my lovely wife, Bernadette, for her confidence in me and assistance with my English grammar; Lea Flanders, for her fine review; Mike Bullock, my talented friend, for his valuable editorial help. And last but not least, I thank my very special friend Dr. Albert Dawson for his encouragement, professional advice and excellent job of editing in giving this book a finishing touch. Without the help and support of all these outstanding individuals, I could not have done it.

My final thanks are to you, the reader, for being interested in the lives of other people in the world, especially the ones who are suffering in the Middle East. It is my sincere hope that through compassionate diplomacy, we can make the world a better place for everyone.

Table of Contents

Preface

Preface

The four main objectives of this book are: (1) to provide pertinent information on Islamic culture and beliefs, which dictate the lives of an ever increasing number of followers, estimated at 1.6 billion, and to show its similarity to Christianity; (2) to explain that "Holy Jihad" against America by *all* Moslems is a threat, not a reality, and that Islam does not promote terrorism; (3) to reveal critical facts about the strategic geographical and cultural importance of the Middle East which have been the source of grave misunderstandings in how we have formulated ill conceived foreign policies; and (4) to recommend how we can establish better policies based on more accurate information and greater sensitivity to other countries, peoples, and cultures.

The tragedy of September 11, 2001 was a warning, a wake-up call to all Americans. It surprised us, just as Pearl Harbor did. Until the shameful destruction of the World Trade Center and attack on the Pentagon by terrorists, most Americans simply were not concerned about the world beyond our shores. We had our own peaceful lives and felt secure not imagining anything so heinous could happen to us here. Because of our military strength and the physical distance from troubled areas many of us were not particularly interested in our foreign policies. World Wars I and II took place primarily in Europe and Asia; the atom bomb destroyed Hiroshima; and the Korean War, Vietnam and Middle East conflicts were fought in far away places. The well thought-out attack by a few Arab terrorists, resulting in the death of some three thousand innocent people in America, proved we are not untouchable and that there is an unhappy world across the ocean.

I believe this devastating attack contained a clear message to our government to be wary of interfering in other countries' affairs if we wish not to become a party to the problem, which has been our tendency in the past. Dictating to other nations how to conduct their lives, especially Islamic countries, which have been vocal in expressing their opposition to us, could result in more serious consequences in the future. We must learn more about other cultures and people in order to make more favorable policies. The best decision our government could make is helping other nations rather than exploiting them for our personal benefit and life style. Sending in military troops and name calling is not the American Way. They only generate more hatred and aggression. If we want to play a meaningful role, as the most powerful nation on earth, we must do so as a valuable friend rather than a big bully.

Just because life is good in America doesn't mean it is the same for the rest of the world. Thousands of innocent people die every day from wars, disease, starvation, torture and terror in many parts of the world, tragedies to which we can no longer turn a blind eye.

Understanding the roots of discontent for other nations incited by starvation - lack of dignity - loss of territory - absence of freedom - military incursions - attacks on religious sites, would help stop the seeds of terrorism. Desperation coupled with poverty produces frustrated, irrational people. The common citizens in Third World countries are the ones most affected by economic sanctions, not the heads of states who have unlimited finances and resources.

Peaceful living with other nations in our global village requires people to recognize other cultures, traditions, religions and limitations. Every country, not just America, is entitled to choose a political system that works best for them. It may not be our choice, but if we are realistic we would know that democracy is not viable for every nation. The concept is wonderful, and maybe one day every country can be democratic, but until people can read and write, the responsibilities which come with democracy cannot be fulfilled.

Desperate, poverty-stricken people who are occupied by other countries do not have the financial resources and the influence that their wealthy enemies possess. Therefore, they find terrorism the only way to get their message across.

Terrorism today is the poor man's way to fight powerful adversaries. Continued military efforts on one side and suicide bombing on the other will only ignite deeper resentment, hatred, and retaliation in a never ending battle. A diplomatic approach and a willingness to find, soften or remove the causes for discontent would be the best solution.

Regardless of how powerful America is, we cannot stop terrorism by "killing them all." It may temporarily be held in check in specific areas but not eliminated. Placing a standing army all around the world to exhibit our military might is not a good idea either. A war against terrorism is very similar to the war against illegal drugs or crime. It is a constant battle, which if not addressed properly, is destined to become worse.

Understanding Islam is absolutely necessary in order to formulate better foreign policies for America. *Moslems are not the enemy, nor is the Islam faith; our foreign policies are. Patriotism does not mean closing our eyes to the facts.*

To be a good leader, America must be even handed, neutral and honest regarding other countries to keep trouble out of our own back yard.

The author at the World University Games in Sofia, Bulgaria, 1961 with Valeriy Brumel of Russia (UKR), 1960 Olympic Silver Medalist and 1964 Gold Medalist in the High Jump

1 - A WAKE-UP CALL

To be realistic in dealing with terrorism, we have three choices:

Put our lives on hold and live in fear, thereby giving the terrorists a sense of victory;

Seek revenge with military force and create slogans for the "axis of evil" versus democracy;

Look for a diplomatic solution to this awful madness and react humanely, which is the true American way, responding with intelligence, maturity and patience.

We must be cognizant and ready to face the challenge in a sensitive manner. It is my desire to assist the reader in understanding the reasons behind the tragic September 11, 2001 incident to be prepared for the difficulties ahead in earning peace and security.

Images of destruction flash in front of me constantly. I cannot understand why any Palestinian child should be killed by Israeli bullets nor why an innocent young Israeli could be blown to pieces in a pizza parlor or an internet cafe by a Palestinian suicide bomber. Nor can I figure out why thousands of people were killed in the World Trade Center, Pentagon and other places in our world as victims of terror. What I do know is that America is a world power and the leader of our planet in this century. And leadership brings tremendous burdens and responsibilities.

A true leader should be knowledgeable, wise, fair and impartial. Because we are a super power and have an enjoyable lifestyle which many in the world do not have, we cannot close our eyes to the sufferings of others. Americans must realize that this wealth and abundance should not be taken for granted, as it comes with a heavy price. We must understand our role and burden in being a good leader if we wish to maintain America's self-interest and security.

An intelligent diplomatic approach can hopefully preserve

our lifestyle while assuring that we do not turn into terrorists ourselves. This consequently would prevent mourning the deaths of thousands of young American military personnel on foreign battlefields, and of course more innocent lives as well. We can show the world who the "real" Americans are in spirit and actions to prove our sensitivity. The economic and emotional losses the world has suffered from the inexcusable deaths and terror will long be remembered. Many people have been victims of inhumane and irrational terrorism. But we should not become terrorists ourselves, criminals with no respect for innocent human life by targeting Moslems who simply disagree with us. Our government must evaluate the incidents, learn lessons and try to find the best solution to avoid further destruction and killing. This should never happen in America again nor anywhere in the world.

America has not been successful as a leader in our foreign policies in the past. Our politicians have supported and aided many immoral leaders with contradictory polices. For example we taught Mao Tse Tung and Ho Chi Minh how to fight the Japanese, and later found out that our former "students" had some lessons of their own to teach us.

American government has supported "terror" in numerous countries either directly or indirectly in the name of stopping communism, seeking a balance of power and fighting drugs. For our own self-interests, including oil and combating terrorism, we have done many wrong things. Some examples are: Nicaragua with Somoza, Panama with Noriega, Chile with Pinochet, Iraq with Saddam Hussein, Iran with Shah Pahlavi, Israel with Sharon, and Ireland with the IRA. The list goes on and on with the same outcome. In all cases we ended up with *a short-term gain and a long-term loss*. Perhaps at the peak of the Cold War, when our politicians believed it was the only way to stop communism, our actions could have been justified, but we must not forget that millions lost their lives on both sides in the battles. It is time to consider the consequences of our actions to make better decisions and policies.

As courteous and reserved as Japanese are, when President Bush visited Japan in February 2002 demonstrations against his foreign policies in the name of fighting terrorism were forthright. According to one New Zealand newspaper and a television reporter, for the first time, demonstrators blocked one street holding signs and protesting the visit of a foreign head of state. One of the signs read, "Bush does not run our world."

As a leader and the most powerful nation, we do not have the right to force our relatively modern ideas on people of ancient cultures and expect them to change their way of life and centuries old traditions. We hail ourselves as the leaders of change. Americans, in general, accept change easily whether it be social, fashion, political, religious or moral. Many other countries in the world do not like changes. And if they do accept change, it would happen slowly, because they prefer tradition over new ways. Minority rights, feminism, affirmative action, lesbian and gay issues are a part of our daily lives in America, but these are subjects which are not even talked about in Asian cultures. Perhaps the luxury of having the free time to sit around and debate and discuss these issues simply is not part of their daily lives.

For most Moslems, life is simply surviving from day to day. The majority of Islamic countries live in poverty with an average salary of less than one hundred dollars per month. Many do not have running water in their homes, safe water to drink, clean air to breathe. Dishwashers, washing machines, dryers, cars, TVs and computers, all of which we take for granted, do not have meaning for them. Our children spend more for a snow board, bicycle or a pair of skis than a typical Moslem family earns as an annual salary to feed their entire family.

Their poor living standards should make us realize their reasons for "fighting to die" in comparison to Westerners who

3

"fight to live." For these starving, suffering people, sacrificing their lives for a religious cause to enter Paradise is one of the only ways of escaping their living hell.

The attack on our country on 9/11 certainly was devastating. However, knowing that God or Allah does everything for a reason, we must look at it in a more positive manner. Without question, the shocking incident changed our lives noticeably, but I believe it delivered an important lesson to us as well. It is time to shake America free from our lethargy and rethink our foreign polices. We have been given a needed wake-up call to treat our global neighbors the way we ourselves would like to be treated. In pursuing our self-interests it is great to be able to take, but we must be willing to give equally in return.

2 - WHAT IS ISLAM?

Islam is the name of the religion, and its followers are known as Moslems. With more than 1.6 billion followers today Islam is a vigorous and rapidly growing cultural force around the world. Anyone wishing to understand global affairs will need to know the Islamic civilization in all its permutations. Islam protects people of minority groups, giving them more freedom and privileges than many other religions, which is an important reason for the growing number of black Moslems in the world.

Recognizing and understanding the different beliefs held by Moslems will help us realize that at this time the threat of Holy War against America by Osama bin Laden or others is only a threat and not a reality. That said, I pray that our government will try to understand the issues with Islamic countries and not push all the other Moslem nations into a corner, where they will feel so alienated that out of frustration their only choice will be to strike out.

Please don't kill the messenger, as I am not promoting Islam. I am writing simply as one source of information. I am an American made in Iran. I can comfortably say that I see myself as a liberal, unbiased citizen of the world. Because I lived in Iran for my first 28 years and studied Islam for twelve years in school, I believe that what I have to say is worth listening to and thinking about. Most fundamentalist Moslems will not appreciate my writing, as I point out both the positive and negative aspects of the religion.

In general, religious promoters, regardless of their denomination, would never mention any possible shortcomings in their faith. No one wants to believe there could be anything but infallible truth in their religion. Personally, I respect all religions, as long as the believers do not go to exaggerated extremes in affirming their faith. Theoretically, all religions are supposed to give moral guidance and a sense of community to individuals. In my opinion, we are all going to the same station, just on different trains. It is my sincere hope to provide enough information on Islam to help non-Moslems understand this rapidly growing religion and use this knowledge when addressing global affairs.

Unfortunately most people automatically connect terrorism with Islam. Terrorism is far beyond one religion. No one in his right mind would commit terror. All those individuals, groups and countries using terror as a means to an end, whether they are Jews, Hindus, Moslems or Christians, should be called criminals. It is prejudicial to say only Moslems are terrorists when non-Moslem terrorists operate in Israel, Ireland, Spain, Russia, South America and other countries, including the United States.

I have tried my best to state as simply as possible for the reader the major and important points of Islam and how it effects us and the world. For more detailed information, one should read the Qur'an, which is translated in numerous languages, search the internet, and read accurate materials about Islam. Such an investigation would make us realize that sometimes what is presented in the media and addressed by politicians is misleading. Because of inaccurate information given by our policy makers and thereby creating fear and suspicion, most Americans have many negative feelings towards all Moslems. The lack of knowledge about Islam has created the same misunderstanding about Moslems that exists among the people in the Middle East in their trying to distinguish between the loving, caring Americans and the negative, often hateful, U.S. policies toward them. My hope is that you, the reader, will find this book helpful in easing your mind and encouraging a return to normal life.

Before the creation of monotheistic religions such as Judaism, Christianity, and Islam, people prayed to many gods. In his day Mohammed believed monotheism could be the antidote to the violent tribalism that tore at the Arab world.

Karen Armstrong in <u>A History of God,</u> describes monotheism as: "A single deity who was the force of all worship and who would integrate society as well as the individual." Ironically, since the tighter monotheistic nature of religion of the Middle Ages, more wars have been fought over religion than for any other reason, and more people have been killed in the name of religion than in other forms of conflict and actual wars.

The word Islam itself translates to: submission to God's Will, or Peace. It originates in the word "Salam," which means "to be resigned" and is a common greeting in the region. Islam is against aggression; sanction is given for war only in self-defense. There is no ground for the allegation that Islam is propagated by the sword. The Qur'an states clearly that there is no compulsion in religion. There is no coercion, constraint, driving force, or irrational impulse. Only when the liberty of Moslems, particularly their right of freedom to worship, was threatened did Moslems take sword in hand.

Islam does not interfere in the dogmas of any other moral faith. It has been alleged that a warlike spirit was infused into medieval Christianity by aggressive Islam. However, Islam never invented the rack or the stake for stifling differences of opinions or strangling the human conscience or exterminating heresy. The word "infidel" among Christians means a non-Christian; among Moslems it denotes a non-Moslem, but the term has been changed by some and translated to mean "all non-Moslems shall be killed," which is not in the Qur'an. In Islamic countries such as Iran and Pakistan, infidels are recognized and treated fairly. In Pakistan they are not required to serve in the military nor pay "jizah," meaning they pay lower taxes. Infidels in Iran also are not required to pay taxes, "Zacot," which is used to support the mosques and other Islamic facilities.

Islam is a monotheistic religion in which the supreme deity is Allah, an Arabic word for God, and the chief prophet and founder is Mohammed (570-632 AD).

7

The Qur'an, (Arabic) or Koran (English) is the sacred book of Islam, just as the Bible is the holy book for Christians and the Torah is the literature for Jews. The original Qur'an is written in Arabic and taught in Arabic even in countries, such as Iran, where most of the people do not speak or understand Arabic. The official language of Iran is Farsi; in Pakistan it is Urdu, and in Afghanistan it is Pashto. Many other Islamic countries do not have Arabic as their official language but they learn the Qur'an in Arabic.

Moslems believe Moses, Jesus and Mohammed all were Prophets or Messengers. As Mohammed was the last of the three, his word is accepted as the "Last Word of Allah." The majority of Moslems claim that Mohammed had his first revelation from Allah in Jerusalem, which is why this city is a Moslem holy place, just as it is a holy place for Christians and Jews. What is surprising about Islam and the Qur'an is the degree to which it draws on the same beliefs and stories that appear in the Bible. Allah is the supreme-ruler. He is an "all-knowing, all-powerful and all-merciful being who has created the world and its creatures." He sends messages and laws through prophets to help guide human existence. At a time in the future known only to him, he will bring about the end of the world as the "Day of Judgment," called "Ghia-mat." The importance of funerals and burials, life after death, belief in a heaven and a hell are the same for Moslems as for Jews and Christians.

Adam and Eve, Noah, Abraham, Moses and Jesus are all mentioned in the Qur'an. The concepts of Islam in many ways are a revision and embellishment of Judaic and Christian beliefs. Mosques were built in Arab settlements for Friday prayer and as social gathering places to unite communities, and they served the same functions that churches have throughout the centuries. In an over-all comparison, Islam, Judaism and Christianity are very much alike with a few interesting differences. For instance, Islam allows polygamy but does not permit consumption of

8

alcohol, yet some Moslems drink and then ask Allah for forgiveness. Christianity permits drinking but does not allow polygamy, but some "fool around" and then they too, like their Moslem brethren, seek God's forgiveness.

Mohammed was born in 570 AD in Mecca, Islam's holiest place, and died in 632 AD. He was proclaimed a Prophet and began to teach Allah's message, transforming the culture in 611 AD. His personal power soon attracted enemies, and in 622 AD he moved from Mecca to the safer haven of Medina where he continued his work. His migration to Medina was called HEJIRA and marks the starting date of the Moslem calendar. Twenty-one years mark the period in his life when he had the most influence.

In Moslem belief, the Qur'an contains the revelations made to Mohammed by Allah. The Five Pillars of Islam taught by Mohammed are:

1. "One God"- There is but one God, Allah, and Mohammed is His Messenger.

2. "Prayer, five times a day"- A prayer will only be accepted by Allah if one is without sin. A "minor cleansing" of the hair, face, arms from the elbow to the finger tips and feet must be done with clean water in a documented, strict, ritualistic way before each prayer. A total shower and cleansing of the entire physical body must be done after intercourse.

3. "Ramadan"- Moslems must observe the annual month of Ramadan by fasting from sunrise to sundown to cleanse their internal self, known as "self purification."

4. "Charity" - Concern for and alms given to the needy.

5. "Hajj" - The pilgrimage to Mecca. Every Moslem is expected to make the Hajj at least once, if physically and financially able, in his/her life time. One who has made the pilgrimage is called "Haji," a title of honor.

The Five Pillars of Islam are mandates as important to Moslems as the Ten Commandments are to Christians.

Mohammed had his hands full and a lot of work to do

educating pagan people of that time. However he, like Jesus before him, was able to make them believe in him and follow his commands. To accomplish his goals he demonstrated a great deal of creativity. Scholars who study his teaching cannot help but admire him. Almost all of his philosophical, meaningful declarations and revelations are fascinating rules of life for peace, order and procreation.

There are different denominations within Christianity; the same is true within Islam. The Islamic religion is divided into two sects, the Shiites and the Sunnis, and within the sects there are more divisions and subgroups such as liberals, moderates, fundamentalists and hard-liners. Moslems divided after Mohammed's death. Shiites believed only a "Blood Relative" could be heir apparent to the prophet as the leader of Islam. The Sunnis believed any "Devout follower of Mohammed" was qualified. Today about 85% of all Moslems are Sunnis. Iranians are mostly Shi'ites but Shi'ites can also be found in Iraq, Kuwait, Bahrain, United Arab Emirates, Pakistan, and Lebanon. Some of the Moslem leaders have taken the liberty to interpret the Qur'an to fit their own purposes. I truly believe that none of them had the courtesy to ask Allah or Mohammed for their approval for such interpretations.

Lack of unification, disagreements and dislikes among Moslems are so serious that a threat of a Holy War, in my opinion, could not be a reality. There are significant factors which deeply separate Moslems from each other:

1. Uneven distribution of oil wealth in the region. Some Islamic countries have no oil whatsoever.

2. Shi'ite Moslems in Iran have little in common with Sunni Moslems in Egypt, Iraq, Afghanistan, Saudi Arabia, Pakistan and vice versa.

3. There is no single leader of Islam equivalent to the Pope in Rome to unite the Moslems.

That said, assuming there would be a cause for a Holy War strong enough for Moslems to resolve the three major obstacles, their collective military power does not equal that of the West. During the 1967 War seven of the United Arab Nations lasted only six days against Israel with a substantial loss of territory.

Jihad literally means "struggle" and not war. I have not found Jihad to mean Holy War in the Qur'an, but I am not an expert in the Arabic language or the Qur'an. The "struggle" could also be on a personal level, as a struggle against evil within oneself, or struggle for decency and goodness on a social level. Struggle on the battlefield could be a struggle by violence or a struggle by nonviolent means. There is the small Jihad and the big Jihad. Small Jihad involves violence, for example, defending one's individual rights in a robbery. The big Jihad is a term used mostly for struggle within oneself to overcome personal shortcomings such as jealousy, envy, deception, and other psychological problems related to human behavior. Killing and committing suicide are a sin, unless one is doing it for Allah, not for the late Ayatollah, or Yasser Arafat. The Qur'an did not give anyone the authority to promise (either the suicide bombers, or the young boys sent into battle to discharge mines for Iranian soldiers to advance against the Iraqis, or the Al-qaeda) the keys to Paradise where virgin maidens were plentiful and eagerly waiting.

Islam prescribes honesty and other social virtues. It forbids the use of alcohol, stealing, gambling, and premarital sex to name a few, just as Christianity, Judaism and other religions have their moral guidelines. Islam tolerates polygamy under certain conditions, but if interpreted correctly the practice of polygamy would be virtually impossible. Islam states the virtues of having one wife, but Moslem men during the centuries have skillfully modified the rules to allow additional spouses. Mohammed's conditions regarding polygamy are so clear that based on human behavior it would be very difficult to have more than one wife.

The first condition is equality. It is stated that: "A husband

11

cannot have another wife unless he can treat each wife exactly the same, financially, emotionally, socially and in all other aspects of life. The second condition states that a husband must obtain the first wife's "approval," which in reality would not be easy.

Mohammed knew that it was next to impossible to love and treat more than one wife exactly the same. However, polygamy was allowed to take care of "extra" women, at a time when women had little value in society. It was Mohammed's practical solution for the survival of the human race.

Moslem men translated his caring and thoughtful conditions of equality and permission only in terms of time and money. Therefore wealthy men, who could afford to buy homes of equal price, quality and size claimed that they had treated their wives "equally." Poor men simply divided their small house, or the still poorer nomad divided his single room tent with hanging sheets and called it fair also.

Mohammed promoted women's values in society. He directed men to take care of women, to raise and educate girls at a time when some men were ashamed of having a baby girl and would even bury them alive. He was instrumental in reducing the fighting between tribes by asking them to become blood relatives through marriage. He encouraged men to take temporary wives, "Sigheh," to provide a way for men, who could afford it, to take care of needy widows, especially those with children and no income to raise and educate them. What the Taliban did in burying widows alive in Afghanistan wasn't Islamic by any means. It was an exhibition of inhumanity, not Islam. We must understand the difference.

"Temporary" wives and their children did not receive shares from the father's estate, unless their father thought it was necessary for their education or well being and so specified in his will. This step was to protect the rights of legal wives and children. Another interesting Islamic rule relates to the division of the estate, which entitles sons to two portions compared to one portion for daughters. On reading this, many Westerners will probably think that this is another unfair, unjust act against women in Islamic countries. But we must always keep in mind that Mohammed had a reason. In Islam, culturally and traditionally, males are responsible for the finances in the family. This helpful provision protects the family by providing better financial assets to the son's family and his wives and children.

Another misconception held by some Westerners is that Moslem women are dictated by the Qur'an to cover their hair. It simply is a cultural tradition in most Asian countries, and if one would look back through history, it was fashionable for women to wear hats or scarves for many centuries. Women in India, Israel, Russia, Azerbaijan and followers of the Bahai religion in Iran, who are not Moslems, wear scarves. The reason behind a woman covering her hair is the belief that her hair is the sexiest part of her body. For the sake of modesty her tresses must be covered in public so as not to attract men's attention and lead them into temptation. It is felt that if a woman shaved off her hair, no man would look at her.

In some regions both men and women cover their head with a turban, kefiya, fez, kerchief, scarf, hat or long shawl to protect themselves from the sun, heat, dirt and wind. The burqa, which the Taliban enforced on all Afghani women and which is worn in Saudi Arabia, is not worn in Lebanon, Turkey, Iran, Azerbaijan, Kosovo, etc. There are only two countries which require a woman to cover herself from head to toe. This is a rule made by the government, not by Islam. For practical reasons, women who might otherwise wear a chador but work in the fields, or who are professionals such as doctors and nurses, instead dress themselves modestly in trousers with long sleeved shirts and wear a scarf.

Please do not consider the Taliban as representative of decent Moslems in the world. They committed many wrong acts towards both men and women. Using the goal posts in the

United Nations funded soccer field to hang men and women, as well as forcing women to wear burqas, denying them an education, and preventing them from working, had nothing to do with Islam.

In my opinion, most Asian men do not like the American feminist movement and don't want their females to follow suit. They believe it would ruin their family life as they know it. Women being subservient to men in society is not a Moslem-only practice. It is a tradition based on centuries-old customs. Women are not considered equal to men in Japan, Korea, China, India and Singapore, just to mention a few countries where the people are not Moslem, yet the discrimination exists.

Husbands are the financial providers in families because culturally they are expected to earn more money. But if a wife is a doctor or highly paid professional and brings home more income, the positions would be reversed. It is of utmost importance that one of the parents stay at home and be responsible for providing a warm and healthy family environment. It is considered an absolute necessity for family success. We unfortunately often forget this valuable ingredient in our fast-paced American lives, as both parents run to work in order to bring home more money. In the process our children are often left without proper guidance and the love and security of a family unit.

Divorce is not as common in Islamic countries as it is in Western societies. As the father is the breadwinner, the custody of the children is awarded to him. Moslem women are not so quick to ask for a divorce because they love their children so much and do not want to be separated from them. Also they do not want to be left without financial security.

Although the majority of Moslems in the world live in poverty, many are content because of the amount of love and care they receive at home from their parents, especially from their mothers. Moslem children respect their parents in an admirable way that no amount of money could buy. Those children who come from families with better financial means are successful because of the importance of the family as the center of their culture.

Socially, neither boyfriends nor girlfriends are accepted or welcomed by Moslem parents in their home. However after a couple is formally engaged, with the approval of the parents, they become a part of the family.

Virginity for girls is equated to "family honor." In some countries, a female who has lost her virginity before marriage could be killed by a male family member to save the family honor. Although to many Westerners this is a horrible crime, it isn't necessarily Islamic or exclusively indigenous to the region.

As archaic or puritanical as some of these customs may seem to foreigners, based on cultural, traditional and moral values, the conservative, spiritual Moslems do not want sexually explicit American literature and movies promoted or sold in their countries. The more we market these materials, especially now through the internet, the greater the hate gap becomes for parents towards America. The adults do not want their youth to be influenced in their behavior and attitudes by Hollywood.

Moslems are quite reserved and like to keep their culture the way it is. Their private sexual acts occur behind closed doors, not in public. In male-dominated countries women are not permitted to exhibit sexual desire. They cannot touch, hold or kiss men in public as it is socially prohibited to express affection or flirt in front of others. That said, there are subtle ways for women to catch the eyes of males they are attracted to, such as when dancing with other females, gyrating and swaying in sexual ways showing off their bodies.

To add confusion to understanding the differences, some Moslem hard-liners have changed the interpretation of Islam to such a degree that most of the liberals and moderates of the faith cannot understand it. I tried to read Ayatollah Khomeini's book written in the 1980's, but it was so foreign to me that

15

after a few pages I couldn't continue. Quite a few chapters were dedicated to supposedly clarifying many questions Moslems had in interpreting the Qur'an and Islamic laws. One of his decrees was intended to answer the question, "If a farmer has intercourse with a sheep, would the meat be edible or is it forbidden?" His answer: "That meat is forbidden in the city or village in which the action happened, but it is edible in other cities!" Can you imagine how my eyes rolled?

Ayatollah Khomeini brought with him a set of laws that allowed child marriage, polygamy and wife beating and a legal code that (1) values a woman's testimony at half the worth of a man's, (2) a future domestic life in which a husband can beat a wife, (3) the husband can divorce his wife at whim and get absolute custody of their children. Nine Parts of Desire - The Hidden World of Islam Women - Geraldine Brooks.

Another religious and cultural difference is the eating of pork, which is permitted in the Christian faith but not in Judaism or Islam. Both Moslems and Jews do not eat pork or any of its products. I know two justifications for it but there may be more. One is a health reason in respect to how a pig is raised, and the other is a pig's eating habits which make its meat impure.

It sometimes amazes me to witness ludicrous actions by certain leaders and followers of all religions. History has shown ordinary people, as well as religious leaders, who have acted in the name of God with no direct authority from the Supreme Being. Actions of a small minority, such as the Taliban, must not be reason to discredit an entire faith.

Two young American ladies, Heather Mercer and Dayna Curry, who went to Afghanistan to promote Christianity, are another example. I admire determined youths who perform their spiritual duty as ambassadors of a faith. However, common sense dictates that one should avoid being in the wrong place at the wrong time. They were locked up in jail for months for promoting Christianity in a strictly Moslem

16

country, and were most fortunate that they were not executed for their actions. Ironically, this made them celebrities in America, and they have been appearing on national television. They will probably receive offers to write a book or make a movie about their experiences.

On the flip side of the equation, I wonder how two Taliban wearing turbans and long beards would benefit or be accepted if they came to America and began to proclaim the teachings of the Qur'an to a group of redneck drunks in a bar. I am sure that they would be just as hated as were the two girls in Afghanistan and would be thrown out immediately by not only the bouncer but the patrons as well.

A group of Moslem extremists also were in the wrong place at the wrong time. They went too far in their protest against our government. Their constant request for removal of American military in Saudi Arabia and discontinued support of Israel has been denied for years. The 9/11 suicidal terrorist attack was a direct result of their desperate plea to America. It was a reaction to an action.

This single act of terror is not a significant reason for the majority of decent Moslems in the world to support a Holy War against America. However, abuse of religion for political and personal gains is nothing new. Recent discoveries in March and April 2002 of the sexual molestation of innocent young boys and women by Catholic priests is a perfect example. The blame must be placed on the sick individual and not the Catholic religion. The same should be true for Moslems, as one should not condemn the entire Islamic faith for the actions of a few terrorists.

The problems that American politicians are concerned about, but not admitting publicly, are dangers arising from Islam in the form of religious takeovers, not a Holy War against us. Islamic militants in several countries are very strong, especially in some countries that our government has been calling "allies." I have had my doubts as to whether they are "true" allies and friends. Some countries like Saudi Arabia, Egypt, and Pakistan are prime for Islamic takeovers, which is indeed a serious concern to America. This is a good reason for the United States' wanting to maintain a military presence in Saudi Arabia and other countries in order to keep its foot in the door and prevent any government changes to an Islamic regime.

Our politicians have always said that the reason American troops are in the Middle East is to protect the flow of oil to America. But in my opinion, any country in the region changing to an Islamic regime would be considered a political and strategic defeat by our government. Attitudinal differences between our country and Islamic nations have reached a critical point which are not in the best interests of America. As a matter of fact, the crisis is so dangerous that I am sickened to see that our government officials are not changing their policies to avoid even more serious consequences. This could result in a more devastating terrorist attack on our country. I cannot understand what it would take for American politicians to believe that indeed our country is powerful, but we are not perfect!

The Middle East is of vital interest to Europeans and Americans for economic and political reasons. However, continual unilateral American support of Israel and Ariel Sharon's incursion into Palestinian land will align Europe along with Moslems and the rest of the world against us, which would be a dangerous game to play.

Thinking that American military force is going to stop Islamic takeovers is as wrong as the idea that we are going to stop terrorism completely by killing them all. A number of those countries are like rotten trees. No matter how long and how hard we try to hold them up, because of unrest created by poverty the fall is unavoidable. We can prolong the present situation but their collapse will assuredly come.

One hopeful way to stop Islamic takeovers is to help the citizens economically, educationally and emotionally to get on their feet. We should build schools, hospitals, factories and other places where they can earn more money to have better living conditions. Such assistance will slowly make Moslem nations realize that America is not their enemy. We must prove our sincere friendship to rebuild a sense of long-lost trust in us.

Instead of military clout or secret service activities, America can avoid these takeovers by helping the public to make intelligent decisions, moving away from illiteracy and poverty.

If some countries don't want our help, which I doubt would be the case, then let them be. If they are beyond our help and isolation is what they prefer, then we must grant them their choice and leave them alone. As the proverb says: "You can lead a horse to water but you can't make it drink." It should not be too difficult to understand that if the majority of citizens of a nation choose to have an Islamic regime for their country, it is their decision, not ours.

The Ayatollah Khomeini's takeover in Iran in 1979 against the mighty and powerful Shah is living proof of success for other religious leaders who are determined to take control of their countries. Even with the CIA and American military backing, Khomeini was able to oust the Shah from his Peacock throne. There are many copycats in the region.

Under present conditions, the mullahs (Islamic clergymen) are in a unique position for drafting soldiers into their army. At the mosque while conducting Friday prayers they command the men, "Go home, pack your bags and come back to the mosque. We are at war and you must defend your country." This unique draft system works like a charm for Islamic militants making them capable of putting together an army without pay, qualifications, including health requirements, or benefits. The poor illiterate people do so without asking a question or doubting the Mullah. The helpless draftees have no idea who they are fighting or for what reason!

When President Bush, John Ashcroft and Bi Bi Netanyahu

accuse this bedraggled group of "evil people" of fighting against our freedom and democracy, it is not true. Honestly, hardly any one of them know what freedom or democracy means nor where America is. Many do not even know their age because they have no concept of days, months or years, let alone a future.

Please remember: **Not all our enemies are Moslems and not all Moslems are our enemies**. Religions were found centuries ago to lead people in the right moral direction. All religions have the same objectives, unfortunately along the way the message has often been lost.

The following is a press release from Dr. Abdelouahed Belkeziz, secretary-general of the 57-nation Organization of Islamic Conference, which addresses the events that took place in the United States regarding 9/11 and which reveals their position on terrorism. He was shocked and deeply saddened when he heard of those attacks which led to the death and injury of a very large number of innocent American citizens as well as other internationals. Dr. Belkeziz said he was denouncing and condemning those criminal and brutal acts that ran counter to all covenants, humanitarian values and divine religions foremost among which was Islam. He asked President Bush to accept his condolences for the victims of those savage acts.

"Our tolerant Islamic religion highly prizes the sanctity of human life and considers the willful killing of a single soul as tantamount to killing humanity at large," stated Dr. Belkeziz.

Dr. Belkeziz added that on this sad occasion, he was asking the American President, Administration and people to accept his heartfelt condolences over the national catastrophe that befell their country. He continues, "The hand of severe justice should apprehend the perpetrators as soon as they have been identified with certainty."

The OIC secretary-general also said that "the Islamic world as a whole was sharing the pain and sorrow of the American people in this terrible and devastating ordeal. The Islamic world, denounced and condemned the perpetrators while sympathizing with the innocent victims, their families, their beloved ones and the entire Americans." The OIC had always been adamant in condemning terrorism. True Moslems expect everyone, everywhere, to stand most forcefully against practices committed by those who aim to kill innocent victims as a means to impose their views and achieve their aims.

The Secretary General's stance was reaffirmed in other statements released to the press on October 1, 2001 in which the terrorists attacks were once again strongly condemned giving further proof that Islam does not support terrorism.

The Secretary-General stated that those acts are diametrically opposed to the religion and teachings of Islam, which proscribe the unjust taking of a human life and stress the sanctity of human life. Moreover, those acts are in clear contradiction with innumerable resolutions adopted by the Organization of the Islamic Conference which condemn terrorism in all its forms and manifestations and are also in contradiction with the Code of Conduct on Combating International Terrorism and the OIC 1998 Convention on Combating Terrorism, which makes it crystal clear that Islam repudiates and denounces terrorism and exhorts the Member States to "refrain from assisting or supporting terrorists in any way, shape or form, including the harboring of terrorists and granting them financial help or other forms of assistance."

The Secretary-General also reaffirmed his support of the contents of UN Security Council resolutions Nos. 1267, 1333, and 1368 and the UN General Assembly recommendation No. 1/56, which were all adopted unanimously. He urged the Member States to continue to respond positively to the contents of those resolutions and recommendations.

The Secretary-General further expressed his satisfaction at the positive cooperation shown by the Member States with regard to the recent campaign against international terrorism in all its forms and manifestations, but also underscored the need to distinguish the terrorism practiced by groups and individuals from the national resistance of peoples for liberation from occupation and colonialism.

The Secretary-General stressed the willingness of the Organization of the Islamic Conference to participate in any effort aimed at reaching a consensus on the definition of terrorism.

It should be noted also that Mrs. Mary Robinson, the United Nations High Commissioner for Human Rights, has recalled the pioneering role played by Islam since the beginning of the early centuries of its history in enriching human civilization through the noble principles and values it advocated, which contributed to the renaissance in the sciences, arts, and other facets of life, especially in favor of women and children. She extolled the positive contribution of the Islamic States throughout the ages to enriching human civilization through their integration into the international system of the UN, which is working to spread peace and understanding among all the peoples of the world and to secure the respect of human rights without discrimination.

3 - WHAT IS TERRORISM?

Webster's New World Dictionary has two definitions of terrorism:

1. the act of terrorizing; use of force or threats to demoralize, intimidate, and subjugate, especially such use as a political weapon or policy.

2. the demoralization and intimidation produced in this way.

In discussing terrorism, however, it is difficult to leave the motivation out of the definition. I am not talking about whether the cause is just or unjust. My focus is on consensus, consent, absence of consent, legality, absence of legality, constitutionality, absence of constitutionality. Circumstances, causes, locations and motives of individuals who either commit terror or are the victims have given terrorism a much broader meaning. The intentions of the people who are describing terror, such as the media, politicians or observers, have given terrorism a variety of interpretations as well.

I believe we should give another possible definition to terrorism: "The poor man's weapon against powerful adversaries." It is an effective tool in that it takes only a few individuals to intimidate, cause fear and financial losses to a great number of people. Terrorism is one way that the poor make their grievances known to the more powerful. As disgusting as terrorism is, it has been around in some form or another since ancient civilization. The first empires maintained their power over the people by force, fear and terror. Terrorism has been used by Assyrians, Babylonians, Romans, Moslems, Christians, Jews, Mongolians, Greeks, Turks, and Persians, known as the most benevolent of the Ancient World, but who still exercised force in maintaining control. Terrorism normally has a smaller success rate when it is countered, but I do not believe that it can be eliminated, as we do not live in a perfect world in which someone will not have a grievance.

23

In seeking to find a comprehensive definition of terrorism I came to the conclusion that there are eight kinds. All result from a definite cause and there is no way we can stop them all by war, rooting out the perpetrators to bring them to justice or by killing every one of them, impossible in itself.

First is state terrorism.

Second is religious terrorism: terrorism inspired by religion, Catholics killing Protestants, Sunnis killing Shiites, Moslems killing Jews, and vice versa.

Third is Criminal Terrorism: Mafia, drugs and gangs.

Fourth is the terror committed by people who are mentally sick. Their terrorism originates in their illness or in their seeking some kind of notoriety.

Fifth is Political Terrorism: instigated by private groups, be they Indian, Vietnamese, Algerian, Israeli, Palestinian, Baader-Meinhof, the Red Brigade, neo-Nazi skinheads or Tim McVeigh and John Nichols blowing up the federal building in Oklahoma City.

Sixth is Oppositional Terrorism: as when one cannot tolerate a father's or husband's abuse.

Seventh is Copy Cat Terrorism: such as pathological groups or individuals imitating others. The well-publicized Beirut hijacking of a TWA plane fueled additional hijacking attempts at nine American airports afterward. What happened at Columbine High School in Colorado was copied in Oregon, Kentucky and Texas and even in Germany.

Eighth is Victim Terrorism: People held under hostage situations or in a bank robbery. Patty Hearst is an example.

Of the types of terrorism I have mentioned, all we hear about or recognize has been the least important in terms of cost to human lives and human property, which is political terrorism instigated by those who want their voices to be heard. The highest cost to society falls in the realm of state terrorism. The second highest cost has been religious terrorism. Even though we hear plenty about daily terrorism, the religious kind has relatively declined in the twenty-first century.

The question, "Why do we see so much terrorism now?" is answered by, "We now have so much information technology." If a terrorist has a cause, he/she can communicate this cause through radio and television. The news media will all come swarming if you have taken an aircraft and are holding 250 people hostage. The entire world will hear about your cause.

Without doubt the act of September 11, 2001 is related to American involvement in the Middle East and because of our financial and military support of Israel in a complex territorial issue with the Palestinians. This major conflict has been at the world's center of attention since the formation of Israel in 1948. The first modern terrorism was in 1947 when Menachem Begin, later a prime minister of Israel, wanted to pressure England into influencing the United Nations to establish a Jewish state by blowing up a hotel in England, an act which killed more than 230 people, and showed that he meant business. In another incident of terrorism in 1982, Ariel Sharon ordered the killing of three men in Beirut, who were supposed to be the potential witnesses in his trial as a war criminal.

Terrorism reached its pinnacle with the tragic attack on America, killing more than 3,000 people in the World Trade Center, the Pentagon, and the rural field in Pennsylvania. Our response on October 2 was "America at War," and we bombed and continue to bomb Afghanistan in the hopes of destroying the terrorist infrastructure. The same is being done by the Israeli Army in the Palestinian territories. In both cases an infrastructure is being destroyed, but I am not sure if it is solely that of the terrorists. Since April 2002, the number of Palestinian suicide/homicide bombers has only increased snuffing out the life of more innocent Israelis. The entire world is now on alert and terrorism is only spreading.

America's foreign policies regarding Iran, Iraq, Saudi Arabia, Afghanistan, Pakistan, India, Israel, Palestine, Algeria,

Sudan, Somalia, Nicaragua, the Philippines, Korea, Vietnam and other countries has not been acceptable to the majority of citizens in those countries. European and Asian countries in general have been feeling the pressure obliging them to stay away from our government's policies. Many cringe at President Bush's statement, "You are either with us or against us." They do not see the world defined only in black and white or "good versus evil!" Many have interpreted his statement to mean that if they do not ally themselves with America, they are against the principles of democracy, a case which is not true. At times our presidents and government officials have called some countries "Evil" or referred to them as the "Axis of Evil," furthering animosity in an already delicate situation.

During W.W.II we labeled Japan, Germany and Italy as "the axis of evil." In 2002, North Korea, Iraq and Iran have been given this dubious title. Soon Jordan, Egypt and Saudi Arabia may be awarded the same epithet. The Soviet Union was long referred to as the "Evil Empire" by President Reagan, and now Russia along with Japan, Germany and Italy are considered our allies. None of this name calling will earn respect for America. And sadly, wherever people discover our politicians' pattern of lukewarm friendships and inconsistencies, it only reaffirms their existing mistrust.

Moslems have been vocal in expressing strong opposition to us. At present, more Western countries are joining them in support against America's decisions and actions. With all the signals we have been receiving, if our government does not change its foreign policies and does not stop pushing these smaller countries to the point of hopelessness, we could be experiencing additional reactive surprises from the terrorists. Desperate retaliation could be devastating. The gap between our very rich country and the poor nations is at its greatest and rapidly growing. Terrorism is on our doorstep, and it is imperative that our government make the right decisions in fighting it.

We are not blameless: the American government itself has resorted to terrorism. Terrorism has been "justified" in stopping the spread of communism and fighting illegal drugs. Our support of foreign dictators who have no regard for human rights has resulted in terror and death for many innocent people. We selectively ignore some terrorism and choose not to call others, specifically the ones we are involved with, terrorists.

There are many reasons for the escalation of terrorism. Our country's long-term involvement in the Middle East both in supporting and fighting terrorism has been, for the most part, not disclosed to the American public. American military presence in the Middle East has created an ongoing uneasy feeling of fear in the minds of many Moslems, not knowing their intentions or length of deployment.

Another reason is American political interference. The CIA-assisted military coup in Iran in 1953 caused many to resent American involvement. Our financial and military support of Saddam Hussein in 1979 resulted in the death or disfigurement of many innocent citizens of Iraq and Iran. Colonel North's involvement in the Iran/Contra affair in 1981 led to the death of some 30,000 people in Nicaragua. And, one can go on.

America's support of Osama bin Laden, the Taliban and the Northern Alliance in their fight against the Russians in Afghanistan in the 1980's, and statements issued such as: "we want bin Laden dead or alive," has only added to the suspicion by Moslems of American policies. One day bin Laden is a "freedom fighter" and the next day he is a "terrorist" on our Most Wanted List.

Dr. Eqbal Ahmed, a renowned Pakistani scholar, educator and political commentator, in October 1998 several months before his untimely death, gave a seminar at Colorado University in Boulder. He delivered a highly prophetic paper at the conference. In the first part of his speech entitled "Genesis of International Terrorism," Dr. Ahmed stated:

"During the 1930's and 1940's the Jewish underground in Palestine was called 'terrorist.' Then new things happened. By 1942 the Holocaust was occurring, and a certain liberal sympathy with the Jewish people had built up in the Western world. At that point, the terrorists of Palestine, who were Zionists, suddenly started to be introduced by 1944-45, as 'freedom fighters.' Then from 1969 to 1990 the Palestine Liberation Organization, the PLO, occupied the center stage as the official terrorist organization. Yasser Arafat was their leader referred to by American journalist, William Safire of *The New York Times*, as the Chief of Terrorism."

At the same time Yasser Arafat was known and respected as a hero by many countries of the Middle East. I noticed a few years later, September 29, 1998, that the former tough, scary looking Yasser Arafat looked like a meek mouse as he stood to the right of President Bill Clinton with Israeli Prime Minister Benjamin Netanyahu standing on the left. Pressure and rapidly changing conditions had changed his appearance. Only a few years earlier, he had a very menacing look about him and a gun hanging from his belt. In April 2002, many people still were calling him a terrorist, although after being confined for more than two weeks to one room in his former headquarters without running water or electricity, to me he looked more like a pathetic old man.

In 1985, President Ronald Reagan received a group of unknown bearded men. After an introduction and formalities he spoke to the press with obvious pride. He pointed toward them and said, "These are the moral equivalents of America's founding fathers." These were the Afghan Mujahideen! They were at the time quite impressive young soldiers, guns hanging on their shoulders, battling the Evil Empire, the Soviet Union. They were the moral equivalent of George Washington and Thomas Jefferson! What irony! I can never forget his words and I am sure there are others who remember this speech as well.

In August 1998, another American President ordered missile strikes from the American navy based in the Indian Ocean in an effort to kill Osama bin Laden and his bearded men in their caves and tunnels, which were built by the United States during the Soviet Union's invasion of Afghanistan. It is not my intention to embarrass anyone or find fault with my country, which I love dearly. I only would like to make a point that talking from both sides of one's mouth makes us look bad in the eyes of the world. It should not be the image we project to other nations.

My purpose of recalling these stories is to show that the matter of defining terrorism is complicated. The meaning of terrorist differs depending on who are the individuals describing it, their motives, and when it is defined. Terrorists change. The terrorist of yesterday is the hero of today, and the hero of yesterday becomes the terrorist of today.

We must recognize the causes to cure the sickness of terror in an effective manner. I compare terrorism to malaria: we can't get rid of it by only spraying in hopes of being able to kill every mosquito in the world. First, we must locate the swamp they are coming from, drain it, and then use the right pesticides to control it. Recognizing the symptoms, manufacturing the proper vaccination and taking preventive measures would be the next step. The breeding ground of terrorism is the pond which humanitarian aid can help drain. Generally, people who have food, shelter, sufficient income and security do not turn to violent terrorism.

Surprisingly, I have found that in almost all documents, books and speeches, people explain or express terrorism emotively and/or polemically in order to arouse our emotions rather than exercise our intelligence.

One example: October 25, 1984, George Shultz, then U.S. Secretary of State, spoke at the New York Park Avenue Synagogue. It was a long speech on terrorism. In the State

Department Bulletin of seven single-spaced pages, there was not a single consistent definition of terrorism. The following are a few statements representing this inconsistency:

Definition number one: *Terrorism is a modern barbarism that we call terrorism.*

Number two is a real eye opener: *Terrorism is a form of political violence.*

Number three: *Terrorism is a threat to Western civilization.*

Number four: *Terrorism is a menace to Western moral values.*

I have heard two more definitions this year from our politicians to add to the list.

Terrorism is a menace to mankind. And saving the best for last:

Islam is Terrorism! Wow! Fascinating definition and global knowledge!

None of these provide us with a real meaning of the word. Anyone who thinks defining terrorism is difficult should think twice about fighting terrorism. Because, in all honesty, fighting it is much harder than defining it!

The Palestinians, who are called by many Westerners the "super terrorists" of our time, were dispossessed of their land in 1948. From 1948 to 1968 they went to every court in the world. They knocked at every door but they became more dispossessed each time. Nobody was listening to their complaints. Finally, they invented a new form of terrorizing the people, airplane hijacking. Between 1968 and 1975 the Palestinian terrorists pulled the world up by its ears. They dragged us out and said: "Listen and listen well, because our problem is not going to just fade away." Some listened but not everyone, including Israel and the United States. The world still hasn't done them justice. They are still under occupation and without a state of their own. As they have never given up their legitimate cause, we by the year 2001 all finally got the message, including the Israelis.

30

I remember Golda Meir, former prime minister of Israel, saying in 1970, "There are no Palestinians." For her they didn't exist. They exist now! We have ignored them to the point of fooling ourselves. This major conflict cannot just be shoved under the rug any farther by thinking that it will eventually go away of its own accord. Palestinians need to be heard and these issues must be settled immediately if we want peace in the world. It is a must and without an amicable agreement no one on the planet will have security and peace.

Most studies show that the majority of the members of the worst terrorist groups in Israel and the West Bank were people who are emigrants from the most anti-Semitic countries of Eastern Europe and Germany. The young Shiites of Lebanon and the Palestinian refugees are battered people. They become very violent because the ghettos from which they come are violent. They use this violence now when there is a clear, identifiable external target, i.e., an enemy about whom they can say, "Yes, this person or country did it to us, so we can strike back."

Our reach has to be global, and extend beyond the speech of George Shultz: "There is no question about our ability to use force where and when it is needed to counter terrorism. There is no geographical limit to our country's power. On a single day missiles hit Afghanistan and Sudan, two countries 2,300 miles apart. And they were hit by missiles belonging to a country roughly 8,000 miles away." It has been the American military way of "reaching global." Mr. Shultz also talked about unbelievable claims of power. "We know where the terrorists are; therefore we know where to hit. We have the means to know. We have the power, instruments of knowledge. We know the difference between terrorists and freedom fighters, and as we look around, we have no trouble telling one from the other."

The right approach in fighting terrorism must include causation. But shortsighted people, such as Mr. Shultz and those who are responsible for initiating responses to terrorism would say, "You don't look at the causes of why some people become terrorists. Cause? What cause?" Why should we be looking for causes or try to be sympathetic to those who would perform a terrorist act? Do we think that terrorists are not human beings? If a group of people is so fed up that they are willing to take their own lives to kill others and force us to listen and feel for their sufferings, there definitely must be a cause, one very well worth learning about to avoid further terrors.

The New York Times, December 18, 1985, reported that the foreign minister of Yugoslavia requested that the Secretary of State, George Schultz, consider the causes of Palestinian terrorism. Our Secretary replied to the visiting foreign minister, while becoming red in the face and pounding on the table, (quoting from the *New York Times)*: "There is no connection with any cause. Period." Why look for causes?

Some of our representatives have referred to terrorism as: "acts of evil and/or a menace to good order to good people." Our President and his advisors, and cabinet members, of whom ninety percent are from the old Kissinger school of politics, make statements such as: "We must stamp them out worldwide." Many countries are aware of our direct involvement in terrorist activities all over the world. Such references in speeches must be avoided because other observers in the world say, "Look who is talking." In contrast, Colin Powell's diplomatic approach is to be admired and his road map for peace should be seriously considered.

If terrorism has only one meaning, how can we feel differently about the terror of any groups which we have officially disapproved and applaud the terror of groups or individuals of whom our officials have approved? The Israeli Army incursion into Palestinian occupied territories in March and April 2002 is definitely "state terror." Cutting off water and food in the name of fighting terrorists is no different than any other kind of terror. Bulldozing ordinary people's homes with tanks given to Israel by America is just as barbaric as a suicide bomber. These all are terrors done by different methods.

According to some calculations, the ratio of people who are killed by state terrorism versus the killing of other kinds of terrorism, which we usually hear about, is literally and conservatively one to one hundred thousand.

Based on American policies during the Cold War, we have secretly or openly sponsored many known terrorist regimes one after the other. On one hand we publicly express sorrow, for the sufferings of the common people while at the same time we underhandedly support their tyrant dictator, who is making their life even more miserable. Our political inconsistencies are bewildering and tragic.

I was amazed by reading Benjamin Netanyahu's book, Fighting Terrorism, an excellent job in writing, but obviously, a very one-sided point of view. His definition of terrorism refers to only Arabs and Moslems, because his book is about himself and Israel. I was disappointed with Mr. Netanyahu for his portrayal of Islam as fundamentally at odds with the core values of the West. He also wrote that it is a must for democratic nations collectively to follow his proposal to free the world from "terrorism," which is basically to kill them all. Truthfully, his expression was a close minded, prejudiced point of view.

Even though Mr. Netanyahu is the former prime minister of Israel, he truly resembles others in politics who never believe they could be wrong. And when they realize their actions were inappropriate, apologizing, a sign of greatness, would not be found in their vocabulary. If his means of fighting terrorism were right, we would not be in the mess we are in now.

Following are direct quotes from Mr. Netanyahu's book and his definition of terrorism to demonstrate how he feels about Moslems in general:

"Terrorism is defined neither by the identity of its

perpetrators nor by the cause they espouse. Rather, it is defined by the nature of the act. Terrorism is the deliberate attack on innocent civilians. In this it must be distinguished from legitimate acts of war that target combatants and may unintentionally harm civilians.

When the British bombed the Copenhagen Gestapo headquarters in 1944 and one of their bombs unintentionally struck a children's hospital, that was a tragedy but it was not terrorism. When a few weeks ago Israel fired a missile that killed two Hamas arch-terrorists and two Palestinian children who were playing nearby were tragically struck down, that was not terrorism.

Terrorists do not *unintentionally* harm civilians. They *deliberately* murder, maim, and menace civilians - as many as possible.

No cause, no grievance, no apology can ever justify terrorism. Terrorism against America, Israel, Spain, Great Britain, Russia, or any place else is all part of the same evil and must be treated as such. It is time to establish a fixed principle for the international community. Any cause that uses terrorism to advance its aims will not be rewarded. On the contrary, it will be punished and placed beyond the pale.

Armed with this moral clarity in *defining* terrorism, we must possess an equal moral clarity in *fighting* it. If we include Iran, Syria and the Palestinian Authority in the coalition to fight terror - even though they currently harbor, sponsor, and dispatch terrorists - then the alliance against terror will be defeated from within."

Perhaps we may achieve a short-term objective of destroying one terrorist fiefdom, but this will preclude the possibility of overall victory. Such a coalition will melt down because of its own internal contradictions. We might win a battle. We will certainly lose the war. He also states:

"These regimes, like all terrorists states, must be given a

34

forthright demand: Stop terrorism, permanently, or you will face the wrath of the free world- through harsh and sustained political, economic, and military sanctions.

Obviously, some of these regimes will scramble in fear and issue platitudes about their opposition to terror, just as Arafat's Palestinian Authority, Iran, and Syria did, while they keep their terror apparatus intact. We should not be fooled. These regimes are already on the US lists of states supporting terrorism - and if they are not, they should be.

To win this war, we must fight on many fronts. The most obvious one is direct military action against the terrorists themselves. Israel's policy of preemptively striking at those who seek to murder its people is, I believe, better understood today and requires no further elaboration.

We must impose the most punishing diplomatic, economic, and military sanctions on all terrorist states."
Fighting Terrorism - BiBi Netanyahu."

Mr. Netanyahu continues with his biased ideas, especially about Iran where the people are struggling economically, politically and emotionally from the setbacks of the Shah, the former involvement of the American CIA and the Ayatollah. The Iranians should be commended for their daily fight for survival and democracy, but instead this is Mr. Netanyahu's suggestion:

"Iran will have to dismantle a worldwide network of terrorism and incitement based in Tehran. Syria will have to shut down Hizballah and the dozen terrorists organizations that operate freely in Damascus and Lebanon. The Palestinians will have to crush Hamas and Islamic Jihad, close down their suicide factories and training grounds, break up the terrorists groups of Fatah and Tanzin, and cease the endless incitement to violence."

Mr. Netanyahu is a true double-talking politician. He never mentioned anything about Israel secretly selling arms to the Ayatollah during the hostage crisis when Iran was holding fifty-two Americans hostage and the U.S. had economic sanctions imposed against Iran. Israel in disregard of America's efforts to have the hostages released, always pretending to be America's friend, at the same time was supplying the Ayatollah Khomeini with plane loads of American military hardware. This was not a one time transfer and sale of weapons. It continued for several years during the Iran-Iraq War. Neutral Switzerland was used as a base for these transactions.

Ted Koppel had a revealing and thought-provoking documentary on ABC, Nightline in 1981 discussing with the Israeli administration this behind-the-back arms for sale. One of their government officials bluntly answered Mr. Koppel, who had a difficult time understanding why Israel would sell American weapons to our enemy. The official stated: "We have 52,000 Jews living in Iran, which one should we be concerned about, your 52 hostages or our 52,000 Jews?" This bold declaration shocked me, knowing that their transaction was more for making money than anything else. Netanyahu knows how to arouse sympathy from our politicians by bringing Iran into his book about fighting terrorism, conveniently forgetting that Israel used to sell arms to a country which he now labels terrorist.

In "Cycle of Violence" - MSNBC - March 7, 2002 Ariel Sharon states: " The aim is to increase the number of losses on the other side. Only after they have been battered will we be able to conduct talks. This will be an aggressive and continuous campaign without let up, and when the other side understands that it can not achieve anything through terror, it will be easier to enter negotiations."

Colin Powell, U.S. secretary of States answers:
"You can't declare war against the Palestinians and see how many Palestinians you can kill. I don't know if that leads us anywhere."

This is not the first time America has called on Sharon to reevaluate his strategy; however, the government is not backing up the rhetoric with any kind of serious diplomacy.

Following are quotes from an American living in Pakistan, a Palestinian news reporter, a former American CIA officer, an Israeli newspaper reporter, and President Bush. Need I say, all give different points of views and new perspectives on terrorism:

A dear American friend of mine, Patrice Ahmad, who has been living in Pakistan for almost two years and who previously worked at the World Trade Center in the early 1990s, expressed her thoughts in an e-mail, which I thought well worth sharing:

"The people who perpetrated the unimaginable act of terrorism on 9/11 don't care that America is a "Democratic, free nation." They don't care that the majority of its population are Christian. They are upset because they feel American policy has detrimentally affected their lives. The perpetrators would feel the same if America was a military dictatorship and its policies had a negative or harmful impact on their lives as they have seen it. If Americans were Buddhist and the attackers believed the policy of this Buddhist nation had made their lives miserable, the response would be similar.

The fact isn't the East against the West, Christianity against Islam. It isn't about America being free. It is about people of minority feeling their rights have been stomped upon and violated again and again due to the policies of another country. Our government would like everyone to think this is about freedom, as they don't want to admit any errors in their past World policy. It is easy for the majority of the U.S. population to accept these explanations because most of us don't want to acknowledge our "bad side." This is called human nature. It is far easier to say, "We are the best! We haven't done **anything wrong**."

We must continuously listen, communicate, learn and evaluate ourselves objectively so we can forge innovative policies that are fair to all. This is my humble over-simplification of a very complex issue, but I believe it is worth thinking about. I pray for a true and better understanding among the people of this Earth, tolerance between them, peaceful settlement of their differences and fair treatment for everyone.

Hisham Melhem, Palestinian *As-Safir* Newspaper - March 7, 2002 - stated:

"Sharon never believed in any peace agreement. This is the man that the Palestinians have known for years as well as many Europeans. His declaration was not surprising at all. Sharon has been a controversial figure in Israel. Half of the Israeli population rejected him in the past and found him to be guilty in the massacre of Sakhnin by an Israeli board of inquiry. He was going to be put on trial in Europe."

Unfortunately, the United States government has to live now with its statements and pronouncements of last year. The U.S. was very fuzzy and friendly toward Ariel Sharon and he of course interpreted this as being given a carte blanche from Washington. They now realize that this man could plunge the whole region into conflict.

Regretfully, President Bush met with him four times over one year but at the same time refused to meet with Yasser Arafat. He said that they should talk with each other but Bush did not meet with the Palestinian leader. Ariel Sharon was made to feel that he had the American administration to support his policies of killing them all to end the terrorism.

Michael Swetman, former CIA officer and agent to the former President Bush, said: "Measuring Success on the War on Terrorism is hard because it is broad, just as the War on Crime and the War on Drugs is. We need to get bin Laden and his lieutenants."

In "Mideast Crisis," Janine Zacharia, *The Jerusalem Post*, March 7, 2002 declared:

"People are very confused in Israel. They know that this military tactic of killing as many people as you can is not going to work. There will only be more militance and terrorists who will strike back. On the other hand there are others including Netanyahu, who say we must strike back in the West Bank. He's in a tough position because he is the head of the coalition and has to represent both sides."

President George W. Bush, speaking to U.S. troops in Fayetteville, NC (Ft. Bragg) on March 15, 2002 proclaimed: "America will not relent until global terrorism is destroyed. The best way to stop terrorism is to unleash the mighty military, hunt them down and bring them to justice."

Likewise the President has focused the bulk of his criticism on Yasser Arafat, disregarding a fact that it takes "two to tango" and the Palestinian rage at this time is out of Arafat's control. Unfortunately, President Bush is dealing with two equally strong-willed, old, military men who have been at each other's throats for a lifetime.

The President called this, *"defense liberty."* He asked for a 48 billion dollar increase in defense spending, an increase that included a pay raise for the military. In the same speech, he made another statement which confused me as to his understanding of which was America's real strength, the military power or the American people, when he said: "The strength of America is not the military. The true strength of America is the hearts and souls of the American citizens."

The fact that is bothering me the most in fighting terrorism is the lack of knowledge that our politicians, the President, cabinet members and advisors, have about their opponents. Either Washington does not want to give credit to Al-Qaeda's capabilities, intelligence and dedication or they are unaware of the caliber of the people they are facing. I respect Netanyahu's education and dedication, but I am very sorry to say that he and other leaders do not recognize nor accept the caliber of their enemies.

First of all, Al-Qaeda is such a strong organization that bombing Afghanistan to the ground, plus five more countries in the region, is not going to finish the job. Osama bin Laden is only one of the many extremely capable leaders in that group. There are more than thirty, thus, with or without him, stopping their organization is not an easy job, if even possible. During the last eight months, as of late June 2002, heavy and serious bombing of Afghanistan has not allowed us to capture any of their major leaders.

In addition, killing bin Laden would not be the end of terrorism by any means. It could very well be the cause to ignite additional fires in America. The Al-Qaeda are very experienced and know exactly how to stay one step ahead of their opponents. We cannot view them as a bunch of unintelligent, helpless individuals. They knew that the first thing America would do in response to the 9/11 attack would be to freeze their bank accounts. Therefore, six months prior, they transferred their money into jewelry, especially diamonds, knowing it could not be frozen or traced.

Some very valuable advice was given to me by my grandmother: *"Never ever underestimate the power of your enemy."* With all the military strength and money that Israel possesses, the conflict goes on and is worse than ever.

We must take time to realize with whom we are dealing. In conclusion, I would describe bin Laden as five people in one:
* He is as vicious a killer as Charles Manson.
* He has the brain of Bill Gates.
* He is as wealthy as the late Shah of Iran.
* He is as charismatic as Bill Clinton to his followers.
* He has for the Arab world the stage presence and dramatic duplicity of Ronald Reagan.

People of such multifaceted talents and resources are not

to be taken lightly. His followers will not turn him in for any amount of money. Besides, he is so dedicated to his cause that it would not surprise me if he would have a member of his group turn him in for more free publicity to become a martyr. Let us not forget that his followers would receive the $25,000,000 reward offered for turning him in dead or alive. Then, Al-Qaeda would have American taxpayer money with which to fight us. Would that not be a kick in our face?

Ted Koppel, ABC Nightline, in March 2002 had a special program about an Al-Qaeda manual, a guidebook of 180 pages on "holy war," found in an apartment in Manchester, England. Experts say that it is an exceptional manual and there is nothing like it. The stated goal was "the overthrow of the godless regimes and their replacement with an Islamic regime."

Their message was: "Gather information about the enemy, the land, the installations, and the neighbors. Assassinate all personnel, destroy the embassies and attack vital economic centers."

Instructions for Al-Qaeda when captured were: "Lie about identity, use aliases, and never carry personal items so when captured no one would know your real identity. Winning the battle is dependent on knowing the enemies' secrets, movements and plans. It is possible to gather at least 80 per cent of information about the enemy from public sources, newspapers, books, periodicals, official publications and every broadcast."

Mr. Koppel's guest was Robert Baer, a CIA officer for 21 years who retired from the service in 1997 and who had been stationed in several countries in the Middle East. Mr. Baer recently published his best-selling memoir, See No Evil, the true story of a ground soldier fighting terrorism. Mr. Koppel asked Mr. Baer, "How can it be that we are holding a man for more than a month and we don't know who we are holding?" Mr. Baer's reply was, "He probably lived under an alias and most likely none of his colleagues knew his true name. You can't blame the CIA for not finding anything in his apartment from their search. They are professionals. They compartmentalize information. It is very difficult." Then he added, "I followed people for 20 years who changed their name once a week."

Question by Mr. Koppel: "Why do you think that the CIA or our agencies thought that they had the right man, but only found out after more than a month, that he was not.?"

Answer from Mr. Baer: "They probably had incomplete information, it has happened before or he could be using other names. They are professionals and frankly they beat us."

Question: "Are you telling me that they are better than us?"

Answer: "Yes, I have seen that manual. The sophistication of it is incredible. They hold their offices in a much tighter situation than what we did in the CIA. They don't even know each other's names. Much of the information they need is available from public records and the internet. The person who wrote this manuel is not an amateur. It is very sophisticated. It is a remarkable piece of art. If the CIA would have done things their way, we wouldn't have been caught as often. If these people operate the way this manual instructs, America has to do a much better job. They have compiled information from every good source. They quote Harry Truman, they quote the CIA, they probably have some of their information from the KGB."

Question: "Do you think that they take lessons from us, but they are better than we are?" Answer: "Yes, the manual says you must be prepared to die to carry out a mission. It shows they are very committed. Our agents aren't ready to die, they only work for the CIA. Compared to any Western intelligence techniques, this manual is teaching them to be practically invisible. They have to be able to handle traumas such as killing one or all of their comrades. It is very clear that with our intelligence service, America often is not getting the clear story."

I hope the reader will not interpret my views as praising terrorists or being anti-American. I see myself as a very patriotic American; however, patriotism cannot blind us. I am neither an Arab nor a Jew. I am an American born in an Islamic country and a knowledgeable educator on Moslems and their beliefs. I do not practice Islam or any other religion, but I respect every one of them without prejudice. I pray that the killing will stop and that we all can enjoy this wonderful planet without fear and destruction. I have tried to provide factual, truthful information from a neutral position. There is always their side and our side but the truth, as usual, is somewhere in the middle.

While writing this book I read as many books and materials as I could get my hands on to add to my own knowledge. I watched many TV documentaries, reports and news both in the U.S. and abroad. I wanted to compile helpful information, in addition to my personal observations and ideas, to provide a helpful source in understanding the complex subject of terrorism. I look at 9/11 as a scary storm which hit our quiet country. Now we must remove this ominous black cloud from our blue sky to enjoy the sunshine and continue our normal lives. Earthquakes, tornados, bombs could severely damage an entire city or a country; however in time, life must go on for strong, morally determined people without a need to destroy other places with ill-conceived actions.

A diplomatic, political approach in fighting terrorism is more effective than all other options if we wish to have long lasting results. Military action seems satisfying because it gives us a feeling of immediate revenge but it is not a good choice. Accomplishments through military response are quick but they would not last long. I am disappointed to see that President Bush has chosen the least desirable means in dealing with terrorists. Obviously, a "killing them all' approach, which Israel has tried against the Palestinian suicide bombers, has not been successful. As a matter of fact, Israelis are now facing an unbearable situation of fear and insecurity, a position in which America does not need to place itself.

Grandmother Tala with me and my two sisters in 1948

4 - BRIEF HISTORICAL REVIEW

From the 11th century to the end of the 13th European crusaders repeatedly invaded the Middle East. They did this under the auspice of "crusades" to recover the Holy Land from the Moslems. It was war to the death. War to obliteration. Followers of Islam saw them as infidels and invaders because they indiscriminately killed every man, woman and child, destroying everything in their path. People of the Middle East do not forget quickly. Therefore, even though Moslems eventually threw the crusaders out in a total war, they have never forgotten the tragedy and losses. The invasion of the crusaders was followed by the rise of the Turkish Ottoman Empire which wielded power from 1300 to 1918. At its peak, it controlled not only southwest Asia, but much of southeast Europe and northeast Africa, out of which developed vast, stable Islamic territories. Otto Lang in his book "A Bird of Passage" describes the period under the Ottoman Empire in Eastern Europe:

"Occupied and subjugated by the Turks in 1389, the region of Bosnia and Herzegovina in Eastern Europe was ruled for over four hundred years by the Ottoman sultans. For some reason the Turks chose this area to be their stronghold. They proselytized the indigenous population to embrace Islam. They built new mosques and ruthlessly converted most of the existing Christian churches into houses of worship for Allah. A string of formidable Turkish fortresses perched on mountaintops to guard strategic entrances to valleys and mountain passes.

With the collapse of the Ottoman Empire, the major powers of Europe, like voracious foragers, tried to acquire new lands, shuffling small kingdoms and principalities like pawns in an intricate chess game. There was seething and unrest all over Europe and the seeds were planted for W.W.I."

After W.W.I, there was a period referred to by historians as the "Modern World" in which France and Britain assumed the power that the Ottoman Empire once held. France and England took the Middle East under their control and subjected the people to their European culture and technology. Their world view was to look down upon the inhabitants as inferiors. European control during this period initiated additional negative feelings for Moslems toward the West. Political and social power for powerful Europeans became the priority of the time rather than the importance of religion, which before was the major separating factor among nations.

Oil, as the new source of energy, became the dominant new resource. It was a much more efficient source of energy than coal, which most Western countries had been using. This initiated a period in which control of the Middle East became very important, and possession of oil deposits gave a country tremendous power and wealth. England was one of the first countries to take advantage of this "black gold." They took Iranian oil out of the Persian Gulf for decades until 1951, when Dr. Mosaddegh, then prime minister of Iran, took the British to the international court in The Hague and regained ownership.

British indiscriminately called all countries in the Middle East the "Arab Region," even though some were not Arabic, causing more friction with non-Arab countries such as Iran, India, Pakistan and others.

During W.W.II British control of the Arab Region was a hotbed for conflict. After W.W.II, the Russians and the Americans came into this power struggle, creating the beginning of the Cold War. Both Russia and the United States wanted to take control away from England and France, to assert their own power over the Middle East. Countries that were under Russian influence from 1945-1990 automatically became anti-American because of Russia's strong and continuous negative propaganda, and they remain so today. The combination of historical European control of petroleum in the region and

Russia's communistic indoctrination was the reason for people in the Middle East to distrust and hate the West and America.

Establishing a Jewish home was the goal of *Zionism,* which was founded by Theodor Herzl, an Austrian writer, born in Hungary (1860-1904). According to Mitchell Bard, Middle East Conflict, "His *Zionism* was primarily a reaction to anti-Semitism; it was logical to Herzl to conclude that any land that offered an escape from persecution would serve Zionism's aims. As a result, Herzl initially considered establishing the Jewish home in Argentina, and later negotiated with the British about the possibility of settling the Jews in Uganda."

The Balfour Declaration, November 2, 1917, was a statement written by Lord Arthur James Balfour, a British statesman, philosopher and prime minister (1902-05) favoring the establishment in Palestine of a Jewish national home.

In 1948 Israel was created by the United Nations out of a strong sense of guilt once the Nazi death camps were discovered. England at the time had tremendous power and influence in the United Nations, the way the U.S. does today. Thus, they influenced the United Nations to pass a resolution to give the Jews Palestine, creating the present state of Israel. Previous to W.W.II, Jews had not had a homeland for over 2,000 years. Even though history indicates their origin in Israel, they did not have a country of their own. Jerusalem has been a holy city to Christians, Jews and Moslems. Jesus died on the Cross in Jerusalem and Christians can literally walk in his footsteps along the Via Dolorosa. Likewise, no place in the world is holier for Jews than Jerusalem. In the Old City, they stand on 2,000 year-old stones and pray before the Western Wall. For Moslems, the Dome of the Rock in Jerusalem is the place where the Koran says Mohammed ascended to heaven. The creation of Israel gave the Jews a homeland, but now the Palestinians, who had been living there for thousands of years, are the ones without a home. Besides the loss of territory that removed Palestine from the world map, Palestinians lost their

47

freedom, especially after the 1967 war between Israel and the United Arab Nations.

In addition, I would like to share with you another viewpoint, a commentary by Joseph Farah, an Arab American journalist. (2000 WorldNetDaily.com)

Mr. Farah states: " The truth is that Palestine is no more real than Never-Never Land. The first time the name was used was in 70 A.D. when the Romans committed genocide against the Jews, smashed the Temple and declared the land of Israel would be no more. From then on, the name was derived from the Philistines, a Goliathian people conquered by the Jews centuries earlier. It was a way for the Romans to add insult to injury. They also tried to change the name of Jerusalem to Aelia Capitolina, but that had even less staying power."

He continues, "Palestine has never existed, before or since, as an autonomous entity. It was ruled alternately by Rome, by Islamic and Christian crusaders, by the Ottoman Empire and, briefly, by the British after World War I. The British agreed to restore at least part of the land to the Jewish people as their homeland."

Mr. Farah proclaims: "There is no language known as Palestinian. There is no distinct Palestinian culture. There has never been a land known as Palestine governed by Palestinians. Palestinians are Arabs, indistinguishable from Jordanians (another recent invention), Syrians, Lebanese, Iraqis, etc."

According to history, ever since ancient times, there has been a natural friction between the Jews and their neighbors over this land. In the year 2002, the conflict over the ownership of the city of Jerusalem and over the West Bank has become the most critical issue between the parties involved.

Webster's New World Dictionary, Third College Edition, defines Palestine and Israel as:

"**Palestine**: 1: Historical region in South West Asia at the

East end of the Mediterranean comprising parts of modern Israel, Jordan and Egypt, also known as the Holy Land. 2: British mandated territory in the region west of the Jordan River, from 1923 to the establishment of the state of Israel in 1948 by the United Nations.

Israel: 1: Ancient land of the Hebrews at the Southeast of the Mediterranean. 2: Kingdom in the north part of this region, formed 10th century BC by the 10 tribes of Israel that broke with Judah and Benjamin. 3: Country between the Mediterranean Sea and Jordan established 1948 by the United Nations as a Jewish state."

In my opinion, which parallels that of some historians, there was a miscalculation about the outcome of creating the state of Israel. The British, at the time of passing the resolution, thought it was a viable solution because they believed either the Israelis would dominate the Palestinians or vice versa and the problem would fade away. The British theory might have worked but they did not foresee three factors which changed the outcome.

1. Jews in general are intelligent and educated people. From the early days, they have had strong lobbyists in Washington who influence American politicians.

2. The United States' unconditional support of Israel with financial and military aid placed pressure on the Palestinians. The support in recent years has escalated to three billion dollars. The assistance in the previous year was: $1.9 billion plus 97 helicopters and 397 fighter bombers according to ABC news.

3. The defeat of the United Arab Nations by Israel in the 1967 war resulted in loss of more territory for Palestinians, especially in the West Bank. It gave an opportunity to many Jewish immigrants to settle on additional land, small as it might be, but which had previously belonged to Palestinians.

Even though the conflict between Israel and Palestine has been about land/territory, it is now about freedom for

49

Palestinians and security for Israelis. For 35 years, Palestinians haven't been able to go to work, school, pray at a mosque, and so on without Israeli surveillance. For Israelis, their lives have become unbearable because of the constant uncertainty of suicide bombers and the threat of terrorism.

Regarding this situation, the OIC Secretary-General received two reply messages from the Foreign Ministers of Britain and France on the situation in the Occupied Palestinian Territories dated 25 July 2001. The following is a direct copy from the OIC press release:

"British Foreign Secretary Jack Straw has said that Britain deplored settlement activity in the Occupied [Arab] Territories; while France's Foreign Minister Hubert Védrine stressed the importance of the Mitchell Committee report and highlighted his country's endeavors with regard to the full implementation of the recommendations it contained.

Those stances were expressed in two reply messages received by His Excellency Dr. Abdelouahed Belkeziz, the secretary-general of the Organization of the Islamic Conference (OIC) from the two countries' foreign ministers respectively.

Dr. Belkeziz had sent messages to the two foreign ministers as well as to those of the permanent member states of the U.N. Security Council and to the latter organization's secretary-general, once again calling their attention to the grave situation prevailing in the occupied Palestinian territories and the plight of the Palestinian people as a result of Israel's bellicose policies.

The OIC secretary-general urged the five permanent member states of the Security Council to ensure the necessary international protection to the Palestinian people.

In his reply message, British Foreign Secretary Jack Straw reviewed his government's efforts, within the context of the European Union (EU), aimed at putting an end to the violence and the excessive use of foreign force against Palestinians. He also dwelt on the British government's endeavors to prompt both Palestinians and Israelis to carry out the recommendations of the Mitchell Committee report which, in his terms, "showed the way forward."

Mr. Straw said, in his reply: "We deplore settlement activity in the Occupied Territories (including East Jerusalem). It is illegal under international law and an obstacle to peace. This is a position shared by our EU partners and the international community." In this respect, the head of Britain's diplomacy underscored the necessity to freeze the building of settlements and lift the closures, by Israel, of the Palestinian areas. Similarly, he emphasized the necessity to halt violence on the part of the Palestinians.

The foreign secretary also said that the British government supported the right of return and compensation for Palestinian refugees as approved in the UN General Assembly Resolution 194. Furthermore, he clearly mentioned that the Fourth Geneva Convention applied to the Occupied Territories.

In conclusion, Mr. Straw affirmed that peace based on the "land for peace" principle, the end of occupation and giving way to the emergence of a Palestinian State was the only way for Israel to live in security, both now and in the future.

For his part, French Foreign Minister Hubert Védrine said in his message that he shared the OIC secretary-general's preoccupation with the situation in the Middle East. He pointed out that resuming the dialogue and defining the political perspectives would make it possible to break the current deadlock. He added that implementation of what was mentioned in the Mitchell Committee report had become an urgent matter, especially that the said report constituted, in the "optique" of France and the international community as a whole, the only instrument that would make it possible to get out of the impasse.

The foreign minister went on to say in his message to the OIC secretary-general that the deployment of international observers constituted an extension of the Mitchell Committee report to provide the best possible protection for the "Palestinian populations," and that France was in favor of any mechanism of a nature as to contribute to monitoring human rights in the region and protecting the civilian populations."

During the years Israel has occupied Palestine, the Israeli army has killed Palestinians in great numbers. Some Europeans have referred to these killings as, "Israel's human meat-grinding machine." Palestinians do not have an army and thus feel helpless, viewing terrorism as the only way to fight for their freedom. During 2001 and 2002, the problem of the West Bank has become too personal and the wound is too deep in the heart of both parties.

H.J. de Blij and Peter O. Muller in Geography, Realms, Regions and Concepts 2002 stated:

"The West Bank, even after its capture by Israel in 1967, might have become a Palestinian homeland and possible state, but immigration to the area made such a future difficult. In 1977 only 5,000 Jews lived on the West Bank; by 2000 there were almost 200,000 making up about 10% of the population and creating a seemingly inextricable jigsaw of Jewish and Arab settlements."

Brian Williams of MSNBC News in his report from Tel Aviv, February 27, 2002, "Region in Conflict - Living Dangerously," stated: "Sometimes the problem in Israel is not only the Jews against Palestinians. The tension is between Jews and Jews." He interviewed a TV producer, wife and mother of two, living in Israel. She said: "The situation is so awful with the settlers in West Bank that it makes me feel bad to admit I am a Jew." These settlers are made up of very determined Jews, many are armed, even a Rabbi who was a former war protester when he lived in America, was carrying a gun and he said, "I feel terrible to carry a gun but I have to protect my home and family." The female producer believed and said, "The settlers have a cynical view of this situation, which most Jews don't like to openly talk about. Except for a very religious few, all have a price. And if someone offers them a high enough price, they would be gone so fast, it wouldn't be funny."

Palestinians have not stopped their suicidal terror and will not do so as it is a matter of life and death for their people. Anyone living in the same circumstance and exhibiting compassion would understand their situation. As if all the injustice done to Palestinians by Israel in taking their basic freedom away was not enough, Ariel Sharon's act of April, 2002 was no better than what the Taliban did to the Afghans. His army brutally pulled Palestinian men ages 15 to 45 out of their homes, torturing and killing them on the streets. They did not even allow the ambulances to take the wounded to hospitals. They were shooting at anyone on the streets, including American reporters who were in marked media vehicles. Dana Lewis of MSNBC was reported as having been shot while on location. Israel had Palestinian President Yasser Arafat's headquarters bombed and surrounded for several weeks cutting off food, electricity and water. On April 2, 2002 in a television broadcast Ariel Sharon went as far as trying to force Yasser Arafat into exile.

The irony of the matter is that Israel's incursion, destroying the Palestinian infrastructure and their homes, and killing more people will not stop the suicide bombings. In my humble opinion this wrongful act only created a new generation of terrorists.

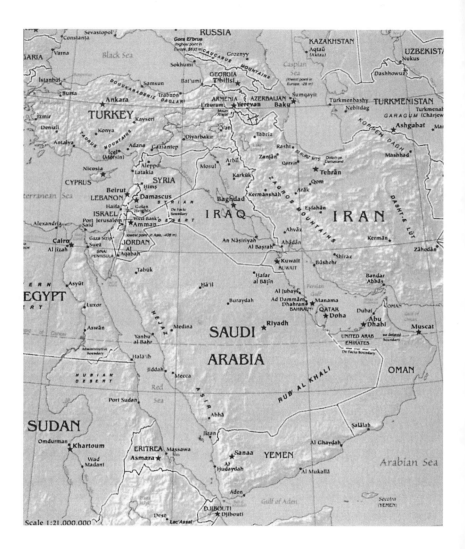

Courtesy of: <u>Yahoo Reference; Educational Factbook</u>

5 - WHAT IS THE MIDDLE EAST?

The geography of the Middle East is as complex as their cultural differences. This region is bordered by Europe, Asia and Africa but unique to itself and with little geographical similarity to any of the three. It is different from any other part of the world, even though, ironically, throughout history, its influences have radiated to practically every part of the globe. It is known as one of humankind's primary source areas as well as the birthplace of three major religions: Islam, Judaism, and Christianity. This part of the world holds much interest for these reasons and because the Middle East hosts continual political, religious and economic turmoil.

The landscape is varied, from the highest of mountains to the most barren of deserts. It has productive farm lands, scenic beauty, mighty rivers and deltas, along with enormous arid wastelands. There is a variety of vegetation and plants, cultivated originally in its soil centuries ago and which now grow from Australia to the Americas. The natural environment and population clusters of the Middle East are varied depending on water supplies, which runs the gamut from plentiful to marginal to non-existing.

Some countries of the region are fortunate to have enormous oil and natural gas reserves which have given them an abundance of wealth and international importance. With the exception of some countries, such as Kuwait, the United Arab Emirates and Israel, unfortunately much of the wealth is controlled by tyrant kings, sheiks or heads of state who commonly leave the citizens in poverty. The widespread corruption in the region leaves what is allocated for improvements of roads, sanitation, education and welfare few financial resources to make a difference. Some examples are Iraq, Iran and the Palestinian refugee camps which have little infrastructure, poor roads, few schools and subsistent living conditions. To make matters worse for many of the peoples of the Middle East, earthquakes are common, destroying what little there is in the way of existing shelter.

The harsh living conditions and extreme poverty have made religion, predominantly Islam, the way of spiritual survival. Islam is now the dominant force in as many as fifty-seven countries. We often think that the majority of Moslems are Arabs; however, in truth, less than twenty percent of the world's Moslems are Arabs. Indonesia has the largest Moslem population in the world and they are as far away from being Arab as one can find.

It is important to mention that the common terminology of the "Arab World," which implies a uniformity, does not exist. The Turks, who originally came from Central Asia, are mostly Moslem, not Arabs, and their language is Turkish. The same is true of the Moslem Iranians, who are Persians, and their language is Farsi. Modern Persian is an official language in Afghanistan and Tajikistan, two examples of other non-Arab Islamic countries.

The Middle East is a loosely defined region which some consider to extend from Morocco to Pakistan. However, for the purposes of writing this book on Islam Versus Terrorism, I have focused on the following countries: Algeria, Tunisia, Libya , Egypt, Sudan, Turkey, Syria, Lebanon, Israel, Jordan, Iran, Iraq, Saudi Arabia, Yemen, Oman, United Arab Emirates, Qatar, Bahrain, Kuwait, Afghanistan and Pakistan. I have written about these countries because they are more problematic both internally and externally and they are currently at the center of global affairs. As you will note, fundamentalist Islam is not the only problem in this region, there are plenty more.

Middle East

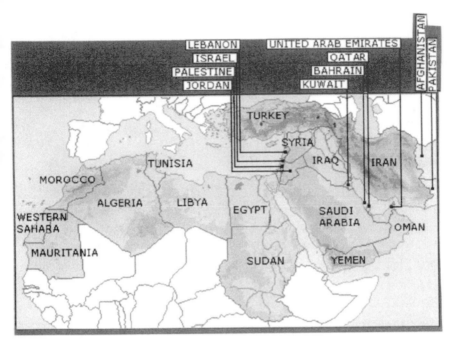

Courtesy of: Yahoo Reference; Educational Factbook

Algeria

Location: Northern Africa, bordering the Mediterranean Sea, between Morocco on the west Tunisia and Libya on the east

Capital: Algiers

Population: 33 million -Infant Mortality Rate (IMR): 44 per 1,000

Size: Slightly less than 3.5 times the size of Texas

Characteristics: (1) an Islamic Republic; (2) ninety-five percent of its foreign exchange is from oil and gas - there is a need to diversify the petroleum-based economy; (3) large-scale unemployment; (4) some fighting continues between the Islamic Salvation Front (ISF) and the army; (5) inadequate supplies of potable water (6) mountainous areas subject to severe earthquakes and mudslides; (7) recently has been used as a communication center for Al-Qaeda.

Tunisia

Location: Northern Africa, on the Mediterranean Sea bordered on the west by Algeria and on the east by Libya
Capital: Tunis
Population: 9.9 million - (IMR = 35/1000)
Size: Smallest of the North African countries - slightly larger than Georgia
Characteristics: (1) government has suppressed Moslem radicals; (2) comparative stability to other countries in the region; (3) has taken a moderate nonaligned stance in its foreign relations; (4) natural resources: petroleum, phosphates, iron ore, lead, zinc, salt, arable land; (5) limited fresh water resources (6) water pollution from raw sewage; (7) strategic location in central Mediterranean; (8) 98% Moslems; (9) import-partners: France, Italy, Germany, Spain, Belgium, U.S.A.; (10) exports-partners: France, Italy, Germany, Belgium, Libya; (11) government: republic.

Libya

Location: On the Mediterranean Sea and bordered on the west by Algeria and Tunisia, on the east by Egypt, on the south by Niger and Chad
Capital: Tripoli
Size: Almost three times bigger than Texas
Population: Relatively small - 5.4 million - IMR = 35/1000
Characteristics: (1) conflict between Arabs and Africans, and Muslims and Christians formed the roots for massive anti-African attacks with the economic downturn in the fall of 2000; (2) oil and natural gas rich country; (3) promotes Arab-Islamic causes abroad; (4) has plenty of dust and sand storms; (5) very limited natural fresh water resources; (6) the Great Manmade

River Project, the largest water development plan in the world, is being built to bring water from large aquifers under the Sahara to coastal cities; (7) Sunni Moslem 97%; (8) government: military dictatorship; (9) socialist-oriented economy; (10) unemployment rate: 30%; (11) imports about 75% of its food.

Egypt

Location: In Northeast Africa, on the Mediterranean and Red Sea and bordered by Libya on the west and Sudan on the South
Capital: Cairo
Size: Slightly more than three times the size of New Mexico
Population: 71.2 million with about 95 percent of the people living within 12 miles of the Nile River or delta - (IMR = 52/1000)
Characteristics: (1) controls the Sinai Peninsula, the only land bridge between Africa and the remainder of the Eastern Hemisphere; (2) controls the Suez Canal, the shortest link between the Indian Ocean and the Mediterranean Sea to the Atlantic Ocean; (3) located in Africa but has a foothold in Asia that gives it a coast overlooking the strategic gulf of Aqaba in the northernmost part of the Red Sea; (4) its history and its pyramids manifesting a continuous civilization which is more than 5,000 years old; (5) flanked by Sudan and Libya where both countries posing challenges to its leadership (6) political ties with Israel ensures foreign aid, but divides its people; (7) government faces a serious Islamic fundamentalist challenge and takeover; (8) Cairo is one of the most important political capitals among the Arab nations; (9) one of the primary centers of Islamic learning.

Sudan

Location: South of Egypt and bordered by Chad, the Red Sea, Ethiopia, Uganda, Zaire and Central africa
Capital: Twin capital Khartoum-Omdurman

Size: More than twice as large as Egypt
Population: 30.8 million - (IMR = 70/1000)
Characteristics: (1) most problematic neighbor to Egypt; (2) during the 1991 Gulf War when Egypt and other Arab countries sided with the United States, Sudan backed Iraq; (3) Sudan is officially an Islamic Republic; (4) a beacon for Islamic militants in the region; (5) per capita income is one of the lowest in the world; (6) a militant Arab African state at war with its own people; (7) has one of the higher infant mortality rates.

Turkey

Location: On the Black Sea and Mediterranean Sea and occupies Asia Minor, shares borders with Iran, Syria, Iraq, Georgia, and Armenia
Capital: Ankara
Population: 67.3 million (IMR = 38/1000)
Size: Slightly larger than Texas
Characteristics: (1) faces rise of Islamic fundamentalism; (2) has ethnic Kurdish problem - one fifth of Turkey's population; (3) human rights issues; (4) cultural and religious conflicts with Alevis (Shi'ites), 20 percent of the population; most of Turkey's 99.8% Moslems are Sunnis; (5) has major territorial problems with Greece over maritime, air, and boundaries over Cyprus off the west coast; (6) problems with Iraq and Syria over water development plans for the Tigris and Euphrates rivers and oil pipelines; (7) importance of location between Europe and the Middle East; (8) strategic location controlling the Turkish Straits (Bosporus, Sea of Marmara, Dardanelles) that link the Black Sea and the Aegean Sea; (9) gateway to Azerbaijan and Turkmenistan; (10) key transit route for Southwest Asian heroin to Western Europe; (11) major Turkish, Iranian, and other international trafficking organizations operate out of Istanbul; (12) laboratories to

convert imported morphine base into heroin are in remote regions of Turkey as well as near Istanbul; (13) government maintains strict controls over areas of legal opium poppy cultivation and output of poppy straw concentrate.

Iran

Location: Bordered on the west by Turkey and Iraq, on the east by Afghanistan and Pakistan, on the north by Turkmenistan, the Caspian Sea, Armenia and Azerbaijan and on the south by the Persian Gulf and Gulf of Oman
Capital: Tehran
Population: 69.4 million with 75% under the age of 25 (IMR = 31/1000)
Size: Slightly larger than Alaska
Characteristics: (1) controls the entire strip of land between the Caspian Sea and the Persian Gulf; (2) major gas and oil producing country; (3) historic enemies are Turkey and Iraq; (4) border problems with Iraq because of Iran's past expansionist days; (5) ninety percent of income comes from petroleum and petroleum products; (6) periodic droughts, floods, dust storms, sandstorms, earthquakes; (7) inadequate supplies of potable water; (8) population below poverty line: 53%; (9) unemployment rate: 25% (2000 est.); (10) inflation rate: 30% (1999 est.); (11) export-partners: Japan, Italy, Greece, France, Spain, South Korea; (12) import-partners: Germany, Italy, Japan, United Arab Emirates, United Kingdom, Belgium; (13) exchange rates: Iranian rials per US $1 is 1,7545-Black Market rate = 7,000 rials to US $1 (Jan. 2000); (14) a non-Arab Islamic Republic; (15) an Empire state over 2,500 years old; (16) respected by Europeans for their diligent efforts since 1997 under the leadership of President Khatami in trying to rebuild their nation economically and politically. At present, more women are serving in the Iranian parliament than we have in Washington.

Iraq

Location: Bordered by six countries; on the north by Turkey, on the east by Iran, on the south by Kuwait and Saudi Arabia , and on the west by Jordan and Syria

Capital: Baghdad

Population: 24.4 million - (IMR = 127/1000 one of the highest in the region)

Size: Same size as California

Characteristics: (1) major oil reserves; (2) powerful dictator - Saddam Hussein; (3) endowed with natural resources - the Tigris and Euphrates Rivers; (4) adversarial relations with neighboring countries; (5) Moslems within the country are divided between Sunnis (14 million) and Shi'ites (10 million); (6) Kurdish problem; (7) pose threat of non-conventional weapons; (8) inflation rate: 135% (1999 est.); (9) import-partners: Russia, France, Egypt, Vietnam (1999); (10) export-partners: Russia, France, China (1999); (11) the United Nations Security Council (UNSC) in 1991 required Iraq to scrap all weapons of mass destruction and long-range missiles and to allow UN verification inspections.

Jordan

Location: Bordered by Israel on the west, Saudi Arabia on the south, and Iraq and Syria on the north

Capital: Amman

Population: 5.4 million - (IMR = 34/1000)

Size: Slightly smaller than Indiana

Characteristics: (1) known as the desert kingdom; (2) inadequate supplies of water and other natural resources; (3) refugees (Arab and Palestinians) outnumber residents by more than two to one; (4) a poor country which has survived because of aid given by the U.S., England and other countries; (5) viewed as a key player in peace process and a moderating influence in the region.

Syria

Location: On the Mediterranean Sea and shares borders with Lebanon, Israel, Jordan, Iraq and Turkey
Capital: Damascus
Population: 17.4 million - (IMR = 35/1000)
Size: Slightly larger than North Dakota
Characteristics: (1) has many problems with Israel because of the loss of the Golan Heights in 1967; (2) a republic since 1963 under a military regime; (3) occupies much of Lebanon; (4) a stagnant and isolated society.

Lebanon

Location: On the Mediterranean Sea and between Israel and Syria
Capital: Beirut - at one time "the Paris of the Middle East"
Population: 4.3 million - (IMR = 35/1000)
Size: Half the size of Israel / smaller than Connecticut
Characteristics: (1) not an Islamic country - one-fourth of the citizens are Christians; (2) Lebanon fell apart in 1975 when a civil war broke out between Moslems and Christians and Beirut was almost destroyed, (3) Beirut remains a divided city with a Christian enclave and a Moslem sector; (4) many Palestinian refugee camps in Lebanon which create tensions and clashes with Israel.

Israel

Location: On the Mediterranean Sea between Egypt and Lebanon
Capital: Jerusalem
Population: 6.4 million - (IMR = 6/1000)
Size: Slightly smaller than New Jersey, among the tiniest nations in the world
Characteristics: (1) key United States ally in the region ever

since its creation; (2) massive foreign aid given by the U.S.; (3) occupation of Palestinian territory; (4) a continuous fragile peace process with its Arab neighbors, who resent the creation of a Jewish state in their midst; (5) their conflict with the Palestinians on the land issue in West Bank and Gaza and opposition for establishment of a Palestinian state has threatened the lives of its entire population for decades as well as the world peace in the twenty-first century.

Kuwait

Location: Between Iraq and Saudi Arabia on the Persian Gulf
Capital: Kuwait
Population: 2.9 million - (IMR = 13/1000)
Size: The same size as Israel (one of the two smallest countries in the region)
Characteristics: (1) major petroleum and gas producer; (2) a very wealthy nation; (3) tensions with neighboring Iraq; (4) limited natural fresh water; (5) important strategic location at the head of the Persian Gulf; (6) has spent more than $5 million to repair oil infrastructure damaged by Iraqis in 1990-91; (7) 85% Moslem (45% Sunni and 40% Shi'ites); (7) government: nominal constitutional monarchy.

Saudi Arabia

Location: On the Persian Gulf and the Red Sea and north of Yemen and Oman, bordered with Iraq and Israel on the north
Capital: Riyadh
Population: 22.9 million - (IMR = 46/1000)
Size: Slightly more than one-fifth the size of the United States
Characteristics: (1) the Arabian Peninsula contains the world's largest concentration of known petroleum resources and approximately one-fourth of the Earth's oil deposits; (2) United States' interests in oil supplies; (3) American military

64

troops stationed in Saudi Arabia to "protect" kingdom; (4) conservative, fundamentalist 100% Moslem population; (5) government - monarchy; (6) legal system based on Islamic Law; (7) death penalty for traffickers; increasing consumption of heroin and cocaine.

Yemen

Location: Borders the Arabian Sea, Gulf of Aden, and Red Sea, between Oman and Saudi Arabia
Capital: Aden
Population: 18 million, hard to determine - (IMR = 75/1000)
Size: Slightly larger than twice the size of Wyoming
Characteristics: (1) long history of border disputes with Saudi Arabia; (2) government is Sunnis but strong 50% Shi'ites creating instability; (3) oil-rich but high rate of unemployment, poverty and IMR; (4) strategic importance for strait of Bob el Mandeb, Red Sea to Gulf of Aden; (5) sided with Iraq in 1995.

United Arab Emirates

Location: Bordering the Gulf of Oman and the Persian Gulf, between Oman and Saudi Arabia
Capital: Abu Dhabi
Population: 2.9 million - (IMR = 16/1000)
Size: Slightly smaller than Maine
Regional Characteristics: (1) natural resources of petroleum and natural gas; (2) U.S. troops deployed to the U.A.E. - air base used for protection of No Fly Zone in Iraq and other interests; (3) strategic location along the southern approaches to the Strait of Hormuz, a vital transit point for world crude oil; (4) consists of seven Arab sheikdoms; (5) official language is Arabic, but English, Hindu, Urdu and Farsi are also spoken; (6) ninety-six percent are Moslems (84% Sunnis and 16% Shi'ites); (7) the Trucial States, now the United Arab Emirates, of the Persian Gulf coast granted the UK control of their

defense and foreign affairs in 19th century treaties. In 1971, six of these states - Abu Zaby, 'Ajman, Al Fujayrah, Ash Shariqah, Dubayy, and Umm al Qaywayn - merged to form the UAE. They were joined in 1972 by Ra's al Khaymah. The UAE's per capita GDP is not far below the GDPs of the leading Western European nations. Its generosity with oil revenues and its moderate foreign policy stance have allowed it to play a vital role in the affairs of the region.

Oman

Location: Southeast coastal region of Arabia, on the Arabian Sea, south of Iran and east of UAE.
Capital: Muscat
Population: 2.6 million - (IMR = 25/1000)
Size: 82,000 - sq. mi.
Characteristics: (1) Strategic location, the Musandam Peninsula, protrudes into the Persian Gulf to form a narrow passage way at the Hormuz Strait between Oman and Iran; (2) ownership of this narrow channel is important because all oil tankers from the other Gulf states must pass through; (3) Saudi Arabia gives them serious troubles; (4) Import-partners: UAE, Japan, UK, U.S. and Germany; (5) export-partners: Japan, China, Thailand, South Korea and U.S.; (6) absolute monarchy.

Qatar

Location: Peninsula bordering the Persian Gulf and Saudi Arabia
Capital: Doha
Population: Slightly over 600,000 - (IMR = 20/1000)
Size: 6,000 sq. mi.
Characteristics: (1) has more than 5%, third largest in the world, of the earth's total proved reserves of natural gas; (2) oil and natural gas revenues enable Qatar to have a per capita income not far below the leading industrial countries of Western

Europe; (3) long-term goals feature development of offshore petroleum and diversification of the economy; (4) if high oil prices continue, Qatar will post its highest ever trade surplus - of more than $4 billion; (5) ninety-five percent Moslems.

Bahrain

Location: Archipelago in the Persian Gulf, east of Saudi Arabia
Capital: Manama
Population: Slightly over 700,000 - (IMR = 8/1000)
Size: Three and a half times the size of Washington D.C.
Characteristics: (1) government is traditional monarchy; (2) 100% Moslem - 25% Sunni and 75% Shi'ite; (3) Shi'ite activists have created sporadic unrest since late 1994; (4) unemployment rate more than 15%; (5) limited natural fresh water.

Pakistan

Location: Southern Asia, bordering the Arabian Sea, between India on the east, Iran and Afghanistan on the west and China on the north
Capital: Islamabad
Population: 159.2 million - one of the world's ten most populous states - (IMR = 91/1000)
Size: About the same as Texas plus Louisiana
Characteristics: (1) nuclear weapons; (2) international dispute with India over the state of Kashmir; (3) internal political disputes; (4) lack foreign aid; (5) Indus River; (6) Moslem 97% (Sunni 77% and Shi'ites 20%), Christian, Hindu, and others 3%; (7) Language: Punjabi 48%, Sindhi 12%, Siraki 10%, Pashto 8%, Urdu 8% (the official language), Balochi 3%, Hindko 2%, Brahui 1%; (8) government: federal republic but is a military dictatorship.

67

Afghanistan

Location: Southern Asia, north and west of Pakistan and east of Iran

Capital: Kabul

Population: 28.1 million - (IMR = 150/1000 the highest rate in the region)

Size: Slightly smaller than Texas / landlocked

Characteristics: (1) world's largest illicit opium producer; (2) major source of hashish; increasing number of heroin - processing laboratories being set up in the country; (3) major political factions in the country profit from drug trade; (4) international support of Islamic militants worldwide by some factions; (5) question over which group should hold Afghanistan's seat in the United Nations; (6) no central government - administered by factions; (7) life expectancy: males - 46.62 years/ females - 45.1 years.

The Palestinian Dilemma: Ever since the creation of Israel in 1948, Arabs who were called Palestinians lost their homeland and they have lived as refugees in other neighboring countries. Israel is now more than 50 years old, and most Palestinians were born after the partition of Palestine in 1948.

Current estimates of Palestinian populations in the region are as follows:

Israel and Occupied Territories:	4,715,000
Jordan	2,540,000
Lebanon	500,000
Syria	443,000
Saudi Arabia	334,000
Iraq	87,000
Egypt	72,000
Kuwait	35,000
Libya	31,000
Other Arab States	570,000

In conclusion, the internal strife, religious factions, poor economies, political struggles, illicit drugs, militant groups, illiteracy, poverty, plus the external conflicts created with border disputes, have kept the region in never-ending turmoil. Furthermore, pollution, contamination of the rivers and seas with raw sewage and oil spills from tankers, shortages of potable water and natural hazards have created such impossible conditions that neither peace nor unity can be expected in the Middle East in the near future. It is a part of the world which is unique to itself. The region continues to baffle me and many others, who like myself, grew up there. I can thus easily understand how the puzzle of the Middle East is confusing to outsiders.

In writing this book, three thoughts have continuously run through my mind:

One: Islam is a pervasive and time-consuming religion continually reminding the faithful of Allah to be stoic in every aspect of their lives, thereby, offering its followers spiritual strength and a diversion from their daily sufferings.

Two: *Inshallah* (God willing!) and *Mashallah* (Thank God!) are two expressions used by Moslems in almost every sentence uttered because they reflect the uncertainty of their lives and their complete resignation to the power of Allah. Most persons when they leave their homes in the morning truly do not know if they will safely return to their families at night. This uncertainty explains why they say *Inshallah* when they leave and *Mashallah* when they return. Whether one is an Israeli going to the market place or a Palestinian praying at home or an Iraqi going to work or a Saudi riding a camel through the desert, one has no control over events or one's life; therefore, everything is stoically put in God's hands. Add to the equation Washington's strategy of fighting terrorism - "we're going to get them all with our military might" - makes them all the more devoted Moslems as they seek protection and refuge from one more threat to their lives.

69

Third: My grandmother, to whom I owe my life, was a wise Moslem and shared with me her philosophy on life: "Never expect life to be perfect". *When you have a lady, you don't have a room. And when you have a room, you cannot find a lady. When you are young and eager to eat, you don't have the money to buy food. When you are old and have the money, you don't have the appetite, teeth, or health to enjoy a meal.*

Such a philosophy on life ironically reminds me today that a poor, nomad Afghani, who does not have food to eat, is in the same predicament as a wealthy, educated Israeli who cannot enjoy a meal in a restaurant without the fear of being blown away by a suicide bomber. Life is indeed insecure in the Middle East!

A LITTLE INTERNATIONAL HUMOR

The following shows our cultural differences and knowledge of geography in a funny, but sad way. A worldwide survey was conducted by the United Nations. It was a simple, single-line questionnaire asking people on the street:

"Would you please give your opinion about the food shortage in the rest of the world." The survey was a huge failure!

* In Africa they did not know what *food* was.
* Western Europeans, didn't know what *shortage* meant.
* In Eastern Europe they had difficulties trying to figure out the meaning of *opinion*
* Drug producing countries of South America did not know what the word *please* meant.
* And the people of the United States didn't know what is *the rest of the world*.

6 - CULTURAL DIFFERENCES

Politicians could formulate better global policies and become more respectable ambassadors if they were sensitive to and knowledgeable about the people of other cultures. We would be viewed more as friends than as capitalists, which is how most Middle Easterners think of us.

Democracy is not a possibility for all 188 nations. To expect a country such as Afghanistan, which has been a nation of warring tribes for centuries, to convert to democracy is about the same as hoping to find ice in the Sahara Desert. As pessimistic as my statement may be interpreted, for some countries only a dictatorship, a socialistic system, or similar forms of government may be practical. Unfortunately, the problem in many countries has been the tyrannical, self-centered leaders, and not necessarily the political system.

Our world is made up of many people with many different personalities. Imagine if we all were the same: one race, one color, one physical shape with one language and one way of behaving. How dull our world would be! We are not identical, and it is our differences which make each one of us and our countries unique. How exciting it is to learn about other nationalities, to study other cultures, and to travel and explore the world in its entirety. Unique and beautiful traditions of many countries are ceremoniously and lovingly passed on from one generation to the next with great honor and reverence.

Let us examine, for instance, the status of the male in Asian societies, a status that is very similar in many countries. In the family, the man is the head of the household and the primary financial provider. In government and in business, men normally hold the senior positions. Their role, their traditions, and their values are not open for negotiation or debate as the female is considered to be the nurturer and caretaker of the family. Thus, one can see that Mid-Eastern views of the world and foreign policies are closely tied to their cultural traditions.

The status of women is probably the most profound single difference between Western and Eastern civilizations. Unless a woman is extremely exceptional, she normally will not be nominated to a position of authority in any of the Asian governments. Indira Gandhi of India and Golda Meir of Israel were two well-known and respected prime ministers and heads of state in their countries, but they were the exceptions.

Madeline Albright, former Secretary of State for President Clinton, is a very intelligent woman and truly quite a remarkable person. As representative of the U.S. she was sent to the Middle East to be a broker of peace between the Israelis and the Palestinians. However, knowing the cultural differences, it is difficult to understand why President Clinton decided to send Ms. Albright to mediate in a region which is known as a "man's world." Out of consideration for a different culture, President Clinton should have sent a male representative if he hoped to gain any degree of success. People in the Middle East interpreted her participation differently. Moslems thought that either our president intended to insult them or that he was disregarding their traditions because of arrogance or ignorance! Whatever the reason, Ms. Albright in their mind set was not the right person for the position. Consequently, we had three strikes against possible success before the game started: (1) She is woman; (2) She is Jewish; and (3) She did not wear a head covering. I hope that American women will not be offended by these observations and conclusions. I am not defending the traditions of the Middle East, nor am I implying that they are right. I am simply stating the fact that the position of women is indeed one of the most striking contrasts between Westerners and Moslem practice which should be considered for successful diplomacy. The following is an example of our wrong attitudes.

Lt. Col. Martha McSally, a USAF pilot stationed in Saudi Arabia, has filed a law suit against the U.S. government, according to NBC reporter Andrea Mitchell, March 2002, for having to adhere to the customs of the country i.e. not drive a car and wear a chador when off base. She wanted to be treated as a soldier, a man, and as an equal, which of course she was accustomed to in the U.S. and in the military.

It was pleasing to see Senator Hillary Clinton on her visit to Israel in March 2002 wearing a scarf while visiting the grave of former Prime Minister Rabin. On the other hand, I thought it struck many as strange to hear her encourage Americans to visit Israel at this particular time, in the middle of a war, to show American support of Jews with no mention of Palestinians, etc. Nothing surprises me anymore when it comes to our politicians and their statements when they are soliciting votes.

The role of grandparents and parents is of utmost importance to Moslems. There is no emancipation age. A son or daughter might be 50 years old, more educated and sophisticated than the parents, but still on important issues he/she will have the courtesy and respect to seek the advice of their father before making an important decision.

The following paragraph, although addressing Chinese culture, also explains the Moslem cultural tradition very well.

"Patterns of obedience are inextricably bound up in Chinese society. Women obey and defer to men. Younger brothers to elder brothers and sons to fathers. Respect flows upwards, from young to old, from subject to ruler. Age is venerated since it gives everything including people, objects and institutions their dignity and worth: The elderly may be at their weakest physically, but they are at their peak of wisdom. The key to family order is filial piety, children's respect for and duty towards their parents. There are strict codes of obedience, as well as the concept of "Face"- to let down the family is a great shame for the Chinese." Quote from the Lonely Planet-China 5th Edition.

It is a misconception to think that Moslem parents force their children into a marriage without consideration of love. Unfortunately, many Moslems live in poverty with large families. If marrying the daughter to an older, wealthier man is the only means of providing food, shelter and clothing for their child, then traditionally and culturally, an arranged marriage in their eyes is the only answer. Marrying for love becomes luxury, most commonly for the rich. Thus it is customary for parents to guide and help their children in marriage, not to force them. Parental involvement helps the young couple to have a more stable family life, resulting in a smaller percentage of divorces. Families in Asia commonly stay together through thick and thin. As a result school drop outs, drug related incidents, sexual diseases, and other problems in general are not as common.

Obviously, there are parents who occasionally misuse their authority and force their child to marry, but they would be among the small minority. Alas, on a personal note my father was one; but he was unjust in many aspects of his children's lives. He forced my sister into a marriage with a man 20 years her senior, whom she detested and later left. My father's actions were not religious nor Islamic; he was just a bad parent. He probably would have been a better human being if he had been a good, practicing Moslem.

Parents, being wiser, are expected to be better judges of character and are generally more successful in selecting a partner for life. In addition, it is believed that, because they are not emotionally involved they will be able to recommend with reason and calmness a more suitable partner than a teenager blinded by passion. The choice of partner is ultimately between the marrying couple, but the final approval of marriage rests with the parents. The established criterion for selecting a mate in Asian tradition is based on common sense rather than physical chemistry. Financial stability for the newlyweds is the most important factor. A gorgeous hunk without money, education or a dependable job might be a great sex partner, but he might not necessarily be able to guarantee a home, food, clothes or schooling for the children. Strong parental involvement is intended to ensure that the daughter and her children are provided with the basic necessities to avoid future hardship.

After the material and financial requirements are met, the next qualities parents look for in a future husband are his character and personality. With this in mind, they evaluate whether he is a moral, stable, and dependable person. When parents are looking at a potential wife for their son, they expect the bride to be moral and able to manage and care for her family. She should be a good mother and role model for children in order to create a happy and successful home life.

From a traditional point of view, taking care of their children, helping them to secure a promising future by selecting the best possible partners for their sons or daughters are at the very heart of Islamic society, the Moslem family and home.

Considering all the above reasons, it is not too difficult to understand why Asian parents are helpful resources and not the antagonists. In my opinion, nothing is wrong with parents having a significant role in evaluating a lifetime partner. That said, of course, not all arranged marriages are successful, because nothing in life is guaranteed. An old Persian saying is, "We need two lives in this world, one to learn in, the other, to use our past experiences."

Even in cases of extreme poverty, when a father has no choice but to relinquish his pride and give his son or daughter to a wealthy family as a servant, it is with the understanding and hope that he is providing his child with a better life. The child's future depends on the decency of the wealthy family. This practice, thoroughly misunderstood in the West, is no different than putting a child up for adoption in any other country. What we see and hear almost exclusively in this country, however, is portrayed in documentaries such as the 1999 Cinemax film titled "The Slaughter of Innocence." This documentary sadly depicts how many innocent, poverty stricken, young girls living in the villages of Nepal were sold to skillful dealers who made a lucrative living by selling the virgin girls in India for prostitution. The dealers came to the homes of the peasant parents and offered them a large amount of money for their daughters with a promise of future monthly payments. The parents were told that their daughters would be servants in big homes in the cities and would be given lodging, food and clothing. The girls, as young as 8 years old, however, were taken away and sold to "madams" in brothels. The lives of these children were absolutely appalling. Many contracted AIDS by the age of 14, and by 18 they were "used up." The unsuspecting parents, who in their hearts thought they had done something wonderful for their daughter, did not know that they had cast their child into ever deeper misery and desperation.

The question we must ask ourselves is the following. How can we determine the right policies concerning other countries, if for nine out of ten U.S. presidents, nonwestern cultures are "foreign?" For the single president who might know something about other nations, the knowledge is either informal, from parents, or is learned from the secret service, which in most cases, has been far from accurate. What exactly qualifies a congressman, senator or a president from Texas, California or Arkansas to have a clear perception of what is best for countries such as Afghanistan, Iran, Russia, Iraq, Pakistan, Korea, Japan and others? This could have been especially true for the president from Arkansas whose expertise was proven to be focused in "under the desk activities," while conducting business by phone with a congressman. All kidding aside, he was probably better informed than some others because he was educated and lived abroad for a period. Too many presidents have had little, if any, exposure to the world beyond our shores. As only one example, George W. Bush didn't know the name of Pakistan's president when running for office in 2000!

The lack of knowledge and the subsequent breakdown in communication and understanding reminds me of a funny, cultural incident I had with an American couple in Tehran. I was driving with three of my best friends for a weekend getaway to the Caspian Sea, a favorite vacation spot. Ten kilometers outside of Tehran I saw a huge crowd gathered around an accident involving a car and taxi. It is quite typical for people in the region, out of curiosity, to gather around any such incident. This time they had a better incentive - a gorgeous blond in a miniskirt. I stopped and asked my buddies to allow me a minute to find out if I could help, which I always did as part of my nature. They didn't mind.

At the scene there was a policeman, a couple of foreigners, and a taxi driver "drunk as a skunk." The male, who looked like the Marlboro man, was yelling in English nonstop. His beautiful blond companion seemed very frightened, either from the crowd or the accident, because she was shaking and crying. The policeman and taxi driver, not understanding a word of English, were responding to the man in Farsi. All were shouting at each other without knowing what the other person was saying.

I offered to help by translating. The "Marlboro man" replied, "My God there is someone in this shit hole who can speak the human language instead of this Chinese mumbo jumbo." His attitude upset me so much that I turned around to go back to my car. The terrified woman, choking from her crying, begged me to come back. She said, "We need your help desperately. My husband, Bob, is so angry that he has lost his manners. Please don't let him discourage you. We would appreciate any help you can give us. My name is Kathy, we are Americans working in Tehran."

I learned from the policeman that the couple was traveling north in their own lane. The drunk taxi driver, going south, swerved across the median and hit them head on. Fortunately, no one was hurt. But, he wanted the "Marlboro" man to pay his fine! Thinking all Americans are rich, the policeman also assumed he had his chance to make a large amount of money.

He had his pad and paper ready, pretending to write a ticket, taking his time, hoping to settle for agreeable cash up front. Kathy, terrified from being in an awkward situation and clueless as to what was going to happen, couldn't let go of my arm. She knew they had violated their contract by driving in Tehran, where they were not supposed to because of their restricted insurance liabilities.

It is typical for people in the Middle East in a heated discussion to all talk at the same time. Bob, the Marlboro man, with his insulting attitude and loud cussing voice, was acting worse. My job as translator became a very difficult task. I knew I was in a touchy situation as I had to be quite the diplomat in order to please all parties. To play it safe, the proper protocol was to give the police officer full priority; otherwise, I could have been paying the largest fine! I asked Bob to calm down and give me a chance to settle things for them. I told him I was experienced in negotiations and knew how to get things done the proper way in that country. The police officer was playing cool, taking his time to cash in his chips.

Bob did not shut up for a second to listen to my advice. Instead, he wanted me to ask the stupid policeman, "What is his fucking problem? The taxi driver was the one at fault for being excessively drunk and driving on the wrong side of the road." He demanded that the policeman make the taxi driver pay for damage to his car. Contrary to what he expected to hear, the officer stated, "How does he think the taxi driver could be at fault? The poor man is drunk!" Then, he asked me to translate to "idiot" Bob that it was his fault. He was the "guilty one," not watching for drunk drivers on the road and should pay for the damages to the taxi, plus a fine for not being a defensive driver.

Imagine my position! It was impossible to explain this logic to a hotheaded big fellow, let alone call him "stupid." In his anger, he grabbed my shirt and choked me to take out his

78

frustration. I was the innocent passerby who was only trying to help, not expecting a childish attack. The blond bombshell wife, still crying hysterically, tried to calm Bob down while asking me to ignore him. She begged me not to leave. "I will do anything for you, if you just get us out of this mess. You name your price and I will pay it," she said.

But Bob made me so angry that I warned him to take his hands off me or I would leave. Having no other alternative, the Marlboro man let go of my shirt. With his improper behavior, the policeman stated: "Besides a large fine, I have to take them to the police station for aggravated assault on an innocent citizen." His remark frightened me so much. Bob was so naive, not to know what could happen to him and his wife if they were taken to a police station in Iran. I was not going to have this on my conscious, knowing that if they went to the Shah's corrupt police station, Kathy's life would never be the same. The chance of her being raped by everyone in the station was undeniable.

I told the Americans that they were in a country where bargaining could be the solution, not logic. I would negotiate with the policeman to agree to the lowest possible amount if Bob would stay out of my way by not making things worse with his temper. I emphasized that if they wanted to resolve the problem without any further complications he would have to let me negotiate for them; otherwise, they could be in a more complicated legal mess than they could handle.

He apologized, realizing he had no other choice. Still mistrusting me, he asked how much I would be getting out of the deal. With that insult, I started walking to my car. Kathy ran after me, hugging and hanging onto me to prevent my departure. Her unacceptable public behavior, groping a man in the street in front of other people, in a Moslem country, shocked the heck out of the crowd! My friends, watching from a distance, didn't know what in the world was happening. The all-male Moslem crowd went wild. I'll never forget their puzzled faces. She persuaded me to go back. Within thirty minutes I settled everything for $50 for the policeman, without a ticket or an official report. The policeman originally wanted $300 equally split between the taxi driver and himself.

After all I did for Bob, instead of thanking me, he asked if I would honestly tell him how much I pocketed out of that deal. His ridiculous out-of-line remark made me realize the meaning of "Ugly American." His wife was humiliated in front of me. I assumed they must have had problems together before, but this one broke the camel's back and she said to Bob, "I am not going in the same car with you." Then she added, "Actually, I don't want to ever see your face again."
Crying hysterically, she turned to me and asked if I would give her a ride home. I answered, "We aren't going to Tehran, we are on our way to the Caspian Sea." She replied, "Who cares, as long as you take me back on your return."

Bob started calling Kathy ugly names, causing her so much embarrassment as to make her walk towards my car without waiting for my answer. My friends didn't know what she was doing, but they had great pleasure opening the door and making space for her in the crowded car. They good naturedly fought over who was going to sit next to her as she practically had to sit on their laps. After her long, scary, unpleasant day of crying, she had a great time with three good-looking Persian men, each vying for her attention.

Another thing one can't be certain of in the Middle East is whether people are telling you what they *really* think. They have a thoroughly theatrical attitude toward life as they are always on stage, acting, and are trained to do so from a tender age. This is very much a part of life and has been handed down for centuries. It's a stratagem for protecting private thoughts and feelings, and has come to be a permanent institution, with a name of its own. In Farsi, it is known as *ketman*.

It is not only tolerated but also has become part of daily behavior as a necessity for survival. It's a permanent game and to succeed, one must be a good actor. My siblings were upset with me for writing some memories I had concerning our abusive father in my book *From Tehran to Twin Lakes*. In my defense I asked them: "Did I lie about him or were my words actual facts?" Their reactions were: "He is our father; you should never say anything like that to strangers!" I also have not been very popular with Iranians for writing the truth about life in Iran as many believed my words, which were true reflections, were demeaning to that country.

Unfortunately too many Americans think negatively of people from the Middle East and of Moslems in general. The most common stigma is that of terrorist; however, there are many other references such as "diaper head," "camel jockey," "sheepherder," "chauvinist," etc. In contrast to these negative epithets, I include the following excerpt from a letter that my wife wrote to a friend in Germany. She happily gave her permission for its inclusion.

"I was drawn to Firooz like a magnet. My previous husband, concerned for my well-being, asked me to reconsider, offering to "pay him off." He "knew" about men from the Middle East; one could always bargain and make a deal.

Against the wishes of my family and friends, all who thought I was out of my mind, we married on September 9, 1990. As you know, my dad was an officer in the Air Force and my mother was born and raised in Europe, so my judgment, fortunately, was based on the person, not his place of birth."

Love, Bernadette

As a teacher it has always been my intent to encourage and inspire my students beyond what they may think is possible to achieve. As a lecturer for Holland America Cruise lines, I strive to excite, stimulate and fascinate my audiences, and in a second language, English! However, encouragement and inspiration were not my own fortune in 1980. Because of the Iranian hostage crisis, and in spite of all my qualifications, I could not get a job because of my place of birth, Iran. I applied to seventy-eight institutions, with no luck. Finally, the seventy-ninth offered me a teaching position which I held until my retirement in 1995, at which time I was given the title of "Most Outstanding Teacher." In America today, I feel fortunate to be considered one of many respected American professionals who were born in a different country.

In conclusion, I feel compelled to support our government during these trying times in keeping America safe from future terrorists. But, in my humble opinion, the advice our President is getting is wrong, and I am afraid it will once again lead America astray. Provocative statements such as: "We are going to get Osama dead or alive. We will win. We will prevail" are viewed as threatening to other countries, and such statements leave us with no options except violent ones. This is not a game with the terrorists. This is serious business. Our enemies, especially the Al- Qaeda organization, are extremely smart, cunning, manipulative and sophisticated. They analyze every word we say, and each action we take, and use them as propaganda against us.

Some of President Bush's remarks are so out of touch with reality that they only further support my conviction of how crucially important it is to know other cultures. As an example, late in 2001, Mr. Bush asked American children to be pen pals with Afghani students by e-mailing them to show them how caring Americans are. Wow, what an idea! Let's jump on it quickly since obviously our President thinks that Afghani children not only have laptop computers, but have access to the internet, a school room, and of course are fluent in a second language. A great majority of Afghani children cannot read or write in their own language, but we are expecting them to communicate in English with our kids as pen pals!

7- AMERICAN FOREIGN POLICIES

I hope that in the name of "War against Terrorism," our government is not going to repeat in Afghanistan or in any other countries of President Bush's so called "Axis of Evil" the same mistakes we made in Vietnam. The Russians call Afghanistan their Vietnam, and the military was only too glad to pack up and leave.

President Bush keeps talking about his desire to unleash American military might against terrorism. His eagerness to use force without thoroughly exploring diplomatic options makes the Europeans believe that the U.S. has a strategy for militarily winning the war against terrorism without displaying sufficient effort in trying to win peace. The U.S. currently spends more on its military than the 10 next most powerful countries combined. It is now an axiom that the overwhelming power of the American military machine has reshaped international affairs. To think that the military is reshaping international affairs!

While traveling in Vietnam in 1998, I picked up a brochure from the War Remnants Museum in Ho Chi Minh City. Included in the pamphlet were disturbing pictures of the war and the following statement by Robert McNamara, former Secretary of Defense under presidents Kennedy and Johnson, from his book IN RETROSPECT -The Tragedy and Lessons of Vietnam. "Yet we were wrong, terribly wrong. We owe it to future generations to explain why."

Based on the Vietnamese brochure translated into English, the following figures represent a part of the terrible effects of war:

* In the Vietnam War, the U.S. government mobilized 6.5 million young people who at different times took part in the conflict.

* The total U.S. Force reached 543,400 men engaged, including 70% of the Army, 60% of the Air Force, 60% of the Marines

and 40% of the Navy.

* 22,000 U.S. plants and factories supplied the war with their products.

* 7,850,000 tons of bombs of all kinds were dropped over Vietnam.

* 75,000,000 liters of defoliants including dioxin were sprayed over croplands, farmlands, forest lands, and villages in the southern part of this country.

* In World War II, the US dropped 2,057,244 tons of bombs over different battlefields.

* In North Vietnam American bombs and bullets destroyed or heavily damaged: 2,923 school buildings from primary schools to colleges; 1,850 hospitals, wards, nurseries; 484 churches, and 465 temples and pagodas. Nearly 3 million Vietnamese were killed, with an additional 4 million injured, and these figures remain incomplete.

* Over 58,000 American military personnel died in the war. According to figures made public by the US government, 352 billion dollars were spent for the Vietnam War.

Yet long-term consequences have not been completely determined in the Vietnam War. In retrospect, this information is not for inciting hatred, but for learning lessons from history: human beings should not tolerate such a disaster happening again, either in Vietnam or anywhere else on our planet. War Remnants Museum brochure, Ho Chi Minh City, Vietnam.

For Europeans the 20th century was a time of unimaginable horror. Since the opening gunshots of August 1914 to the fall of the Berlin Wall in November 1989, Europe has been torn apart by two of the bloodiest wars in history, by industrial genocide, and by two murderous ideologies. For 44 years, the Continent has been divided as never before. The legacy of all this is a deep aversion to, almost a loathing of, military force. For many modern Europeans, war is a ghastly, primitive business. War is a last resort; those ready to use it quickly, or worse, who

84

appear to enjoy it, are not to be trusted. Their history has taught them to be suspicious of any armed force. That's why Secretary of Defense Donald Rumsfeld, a folk hero to some in the U.S., is considered "a swaggeringly dangerous Rambo by many Europeans." (Michael Elliott, *Time Magazine*, March 11, 2002 - Global Agenda).

Europeans commonly do not have a high opinion of John Ashcroft either because he has violated the rules of the Geneva Convention regarding prisoners of war. He has made his own rules by twisting words and giving a different interpretation to the accepted rules. In effect, he has ignored international laws.

There are additional reasons for the gulf existing on key issues between the Bush Administration and Europeans. Europe is closer to the Middle East, and Islam is the fastest-growing religion in the world. Most European countries would like to keep their close economic links to the Middle East, especially Iraq and Iran. Some have a very special historical, economic and human relationship with those nations. They import oil from the Middle East and export European goods and products in return. This is a win-win situation for both sides. Japan and China are profiting and trading with the Middle East as well. Unlike America, these countries deal strictly in business matters without intruding into internal affairs.

The following letter from the OIC Press Release dated February 19, 2001 reflects their reaction to an American/ British military attack on Iraq:

The Recent Attack on the Iraqi Territory
"At a time when the adverse repercussions of the sanctions imposed on Iraq by the UN Security Council had started to gradually find their way towards a resolution through the efforts deployed by the group of States members of the Organization of the Islamic Conference during the Ninth Islamic

Summit Conference, which contributed to achieving a détente in relations between the states of the region that were gradually moving towards truth and reconciliation and lifting the embargo on the Iraqi people, American and British forces took the world by surprise when they led an attack on February 16, 2001, which targeted Iraqi installations and caused victims among the innocent populations.

The Organization of the Islamic Conference condemns this bombardment, which it considers a violation of the resolutions and principles of international legitimacy and of international law. In fact, this unjustified act makes it all the more difficult to find any resolution to the problem, especially in view of the fact that Iraq is preparing to enter negotiations this February 26th with Mr. Kofi Annan, the UN Secretary General, to seek the suspension of the sanctions imposed on it.

The Secretary General of the Organization of the Islamic Conference, Dr. Abdelouahed Belkeziz is following with great concern the repercussions of the attack led by the American and British forces against Iraq. He invites the members of the UN Security Council to organize a comprehensive dialogue between Iraq and the United Nations in order to seek a settlement of all pending issues on sound and proper bases leading to a lifting of the sanctions on Iraq. He requests the Member States of the Organization of the Islamic Conference to initiate contacts with the United States of America and Great Britain with a view to taking all the necessary steps to guarantee the respect of the sovereignty and territorial integrity of Iraq and to put an end to the use of force and to all actions undertaken outside the framework of the Security Council and the United Nations.

The Secretary General of the Organization of the Islamic Conference would like to add that the Organization remains firmly attached to resolution No. 19/9-P (IS) adopted by the Ninth Islamic Summit Conference and to all its provisions."

Washington's record of nation-building in the Moslem world, as well as countries that are non-Islamic, has been quite disturbing. Overthrowing supposedly unfriendly governments and replacing them with compliant ones has not been successful before and will not be in the future. We have consistently ended up with one outcome without exception: *a short-term gain with a long-term loss*. It is incomprehensible to me why our politicians have not learned lessons from our numerous past mistakes. When will we learn from history?

The following is a brief overview of our government's involvement in other countries which supports my opinion about the long-term losses for America in every case. I limit myself to only the dates and situations which I personally remember; however, there are many more.

In 1948 the American government overthrew the old regime in Syria. Since 1963 it has been a republic under a military regime. In 1967 the Golan Heights, part of Syria, was lost to Israel. Thirty-five years later, negotiators are still trying to find a way to arrange the return of all or part of this area to Syria, but there are many problems. Opposition to returning the Golan Heights is strong in Israel because many Jewish settlers have occupied parts of the Golan. Indirectly, America is drawn into this battle because of its alliance with Israel, and this breeds anti-American sentiment among the Syrians.

In 1953 in Iran, Dr. Mohammed Mossaddegh's government was overthrown by the CIA. Dr. Mossaddegh was the champion of the Popular Movement of Iran and the nationalization of Iranian oil. His premiership (1951-1953) was a test of his resolve in defending Iran's political independence and economic interests. In the past century he has been the only chance Iran has had for democracy! The Shah, witnessing the daily demonstrations against him and in support of Mossaddegh, became fearful for his life and fled Iran. Unfortunately, the American CIA planned a successful military coup and brought the Shah back to Iran, reinstating the

87

unwanted Majesty as the "King of Kings." Dr. Mossaddegh was arrested, tried in a military tribunal, and condemned to three years of solitary confinement. He did not survive the torture and died as a defeated old man.

Iranian citizens became so fed up with the Shah's perverted dictatorship that in 1979 they pleaded for the return of the Ayatollah Khomeini. Because of his enormous religious power, it was believed that he would be the only one who could oust the Shah, the CIA and the American military. However, Iranians did not expect him to turn back the clock 100 years! Sadly, Persians have not had the taste of freedom since the time of Mossaddegh.

In 1955 in Egypt, the American government tried to assassinate nationalist President Gammal Abdel Nasser, who upon failure of the plot turned to the Soviets for support.

At present, per all evidence, both Egypt and Saudi Arabia are ripe for radical Islamic takeovers.

In 1958, America put Col. Kassem in power in Iraq, and he too turned into an anti-American fanatic. Years later in 1975 we tried again to change the balance of power in our favor, and were instrumental in placing Saddam Hussein in power. We jumped from the frying pan into the fire with this brilliant move. Because of our discontent about being thrown out of Iran and our hatred of Khomeini for keeping fifty-two Americans hostage, we encouraged Saddam Hussein to start a war against Iran. America supplied Saddam with government loans and with classified military information and sites, which the former Shah had purchased from us. Saddam lost the war, an embarrassment both for himself and America. Our support of Saddam resulted in 700,000 deaths, and an additional 50,000 Iranian young boys (ages 9-14) were left mutilated by detonating land mines as they marched through mine fields in front of advancing regular soldiers.

President Reagan disregarded the economic sanctions placed on Iran by former President Jimmy Carter. He sent Col. Oliver

North to Tehran in 1981 with a Bible to present to Ayatollah Khomeini as a gift of friendship, along with an offer to sell American arms to Iran in their war against Iraq. This country was shocked when the Iran/Contra affair became public news. The American public learned of the sordid deal in which American weapons were sold to Iran at inflated black market prices, and the money sent to the Nicaraguan government to fight the Sandinistas. Some 30,000 Nicaraguans were killed in this American-supported state terror.

In 1967 in Indonesia, with US involvement, President Sukarno was overthrown. Between the actions of the army and the rampant mob, who were Sukarno supporters, 500,000 people were killed.

In 1969 in Libya, America helped a young officer, Muammar Qadaffi, seize power. Then in 1986 we tried to kill him with a missile ordered fired by President Reagan. We missed Qadaffi but killed his four-year-old innocent daughter. Qadaffi is still alive and hating the U.S. more than ever.

In 1983 in Lebanon, American forces intervened in a civil war between the Moslems and the Christians to prop up the Christian government; 240 US Marines died.

In 1991, our former ally Saddam invaded Kuwait. Wanting to protect our interests in the Middle East, we entered into battle, won the war but now continue to fly military missions over Iraq. Yet today Saddam is still in power. Based on Leon Harris' interview (CNN, December 1996) with an American professor born in Iraq, half a million innocent Iraqi children have been killed because of American bombing. This resulted from intentional or unintentional targets hit by U.S. bombs. What could their helpless parents have done to avoid such a tragedy? Absolutely nothing! However, their suffering has created a strong resentment towards America in the minds of the brothers and sisters left behind, their parents and relatives. They have all been scarred for life.

America also intervened in the civil war in Somalia in 1992.

We lost soldiers and quickly made an exit.

In 1996 the United States attempted the creation of a Kurdish mini-state in Iraq. The Kurds, who live in Turkey, Iran and Iraq, are similar to the Palestinians in that they are a people without a country. The problem remains unresolved.

We have been in Afghanistan since October 2001 and, in my opinion, the bombing has only added to the misery of the common populace. Jan Goodwin in the April 2002 issue of *Marie Claire* magazine writes about the ongoing problems in a heartbreaking article, "Afghan Girls Forced to Sell Sex or Starve."

"In the refugee no-man's-land of Pakistan, Afghan virgins as young as 13 are prostituting themselves in a desperate attempt to feed their loved ones. It just might kill them instead. If you read the headlines, the news about Afghanistan is encouraging: There's a fragile peace agreement and a spirit of optimism. Perhaps the biggest symbols of hope are the televised images of female students lining up to go back to school after being denied education by the Taliban.

But the view away from the cameras isn't quite so uplifting. Afghanistan has been systematically destroyed by 23 years of conflict, with an estimated 2 million people dead. The aftermath has left many women and girls powerless. Scores are being forced into prostitution, some preyed upon by men, others either sold or guilted into it by their families, who need to eat. "

An uncertain future, combined with lack of food, medicine and basic necessities, has created in some aspects just as unpleasant a life, or perhaps even worse, than that which they had with the Taliban.

Based on several interviews by my friend Masood Ahmad, it is clear that many Afghanis believe that the Northern Alliance brought more misery and lawlessness to Afghanistan than the

Taliban, a primary reason that the Taliban initially were welcomed. People were tired of the warlord mentality and the fighting amongst the tribes. The Afghanis also said that many of their women had been raped by the invading Northern Alliance.

"Many Afghan women take little comfort in the possibility that the opposition Northern Alliance might someday assume power. Its members also have a poor record when it comes to the treatment of women, including rape, say human rights observers. The Northern Alliance is nothing more than just the Talibans without beards. They are dogs of the same field." *People Magazine,* reported by Peter Noram and Eileen Finan, 4-12-2001.

That said, the U.S. now includes them among our "newest" friends. We are also helping another newfound ally, Russia, by sending our troops to Georgia. This is an historical irony of epic proportions. In the 1980's the U.S. spent billions to oust the Russians from Afghanistan; now, in the war against terrorism, we invite them back to Afghanistan to help us fight bin Laden.

Equally shameful, the US has now conferred its blessing on Russia's attempt to crush the Chechen uprising by echoing Moscow's claim that the insurgents are nothing more than "Islamic terrorists." The next group certain to be demonized by Washington will be the Kashmiri Mujihadeen.

We helped Fidel Castro gain power but we have been opposed to his communist regime ever since.

Our CIA trained Osama and the Taliban, sent them to Afghanistan from Saudi Arabia, built tunnels, and gave them weapons plus billions of dollars to fight the Russians. They were successful. But today, Osama, the Taliban and the Al-Qaeda are our number-one enemies!

The facts I have been writing about can be found in most public information sources.

In November 2001, Mike Wallace on CBS's, 60 Minutes

had an interview with three American CIA agents stationed in the Middle East. Not one of them could speak or understand a word of Arabic. Mr. Wallace found this incredulous. When he questioned their accuracy in reporting firsthand, reliable information to our government, they couldn't give him a straight answer. However, one of them stated that he had his own knowledgeable source, a local man on the street, who spoke English. Brilliant! We make foreign policies based on such dubious information from unreliable sources?

It doesn't take a genius to figure that if the information given to Washington by our secret service agencies is at times inaccurate, decisions made or policies formed will be equally inappropriate. For instance, in 1998 we bombed a pharmaceutical plant in Sudan because the information given to us was that this was a nuclear bomb factory. Valuable information has a price, and it can be too easily bought and sold for the wrong reasons from the person on the street, as well as from the heads of governments and their corrupt high-ranking officials. To rely on street information from debased, poor countries is a risky business indeed.

The countries and people who have experienced losses due to American interference and duplicity have lost their trust in America. They have no desire to deal with us in the same old political way.

When the Soviet Union intervened in Afghanistan in the 1980's, Zia ul-Hag, the military dictator of Pakistan, Afghanistan's neighbor, saw an opportunity to launch a Jihad against the communist Russians, whom Moslems believe to be godless. The United States saw a God-sent opportunity to mobilize one million Moslems against the Russian Evil Empire. American money started pouring in. CIA agents were suddenly everywhere recruiting Moslems to fight in "The Great Jihad." Bin Laden was one of their early prize recruits. He was not only an Arab. He was also a Saudi. He was not only a Saudi. He was a billionaire, willing to put his own money into the cause. Bin Laden campaigned and recruited Moslems to join the Jihad against the communist infidels. He enlisted recruits from Algeria, Sudan, Egypt and Saudi Arabia. Not only Osama bin Laden but Sheik Abdul-Rahman al-Saudias, one of the top Imams in Saudi Arabia, who planned and was convicted of the bombing of the World Trade Center in 1993, was an ally of ours at one time.

The point I am making is first the misuse of the word and meaning of "Jihad," and second, the fact that many of these people who were our friends at one time but turned against us, have been tribal people. The real warlords have a simple code of ethics that consists of two words: loyalty and revenge. You are my friend, you keep your word and I am loyal to you. You break your word; I go on my path of revenge. For Osama and others, America has broken its word. The loyal friend has been betrayed by a covert operation or double dealing with the enemy. The one who swore blood loyalty has betrayed you, and you will do anything for revenge.

Bin Laden feels betrayed by us because we first promised to remove military troops from Saudi Arabia after the Gulf War, which we didn't; and second, there was an understanding that we would help to create a Palestinian state, which we have ignored.

Many Americans wonder why Moslems express hatred towards us. None of our past presidents and government officials would admit that we might have done something which created a negative attitude. Even our President says, "Americans are good people, we know we are good people, we just have to do a better job of advertising it!"

It is amazing that our politicians have not seen the red flags waving in the Middle East! The Gallup Poll taken in six Islamic countries as reported by Keith Miller and aired on MSNBC March 2002 from the Middle East, was mind boggling. Findings indicated that fifty-three percent of the people participating in the poll, including Kuwaitis described America as: " Ruthless,

aggressive, easily provoked, arrogant and biased." Frank
Newport from the Gallup Poll was stunned, and answered
every question by the critics and skeptics, clearing any possible
misunderstanding about the accuracy and validity of the poll.

Quite obviously, the poll indicated that what we think of
ourselves is worlds apart from how other countries see us.
President Bush's response to the poll was, "America must do a
better job of publicizing itself." And according to an article in
the *New Zealand Herald*, February 21, 2002, written by
Rupert Cornwell, "Mr. Bush allocated ten billion dollars to
establish a new agency, Office of Strategic Influence (OSI), as a
major covert news and disinformation campaign to help
Washington win the propaganda war against the terrorists,
especially in the all-important Islamic world. The main target
audience is in the Islamic countries of the Middle East and
Asia, but it may also be directed at Western Europe, where
criticism has grown sharply in recent weeks of the Bush
Administration's strategy to combat terrorism." Reading this
on my way to the airport in Auckland, I was jokingly asked by
the taxi driver, "Do you know that now America has a new
cover-up agency?"

Then I saw another article in the *New Zealand Herald* by
Andrew Buncombe which caught my attention, "FBI wary of
charging suspect over anthrax mail," making me think that
maybe there was something to what the taxi driver was saying.

"The Federal Bureau of Investigation has identified the
man behind last year's fatal anthrax mailings but is dragging
"its feet" over bringing charges because the suspect is a
former government scientist, it was claimed yesterday. The
man allegedly traveled to Britain to post an infected letter
to United States Senate Majority Leader Tom Daschle. Dr.
Barbara Rosenberg, a director with the Federation of
American Scientists, said many scientists working in the
anthrax field were aware of the suspect, who she said had
been questioned at least twice by the authorities. She said

the FBI was reluctant to arrest the scientist because he knew government secrets. It has long been believed that the source of the anthrax was a government laboratory within the U.S. but Rosenberg's comments - made at a conference at Princeton University and reported by the *Trenton Times* newspaper - are the most specific yet. The accusation, many of which are repeated on the federations website, say the man may have worked at the same laboratory - Fort Detrick, Maryland, the American military laboratory near Washington. Most of the genuine and many of the hoax letters were posted from near Trenton, New Jersey about 240 km from Washington and 130 km from New York, where three television stations and a newspaper had staff who contracted the infection. We can draw a likely portrait of the perpetrator as a former Fort Detrick scientist who is now working for a contractor in the Washington D.C. area. He had reasons for travel to Florida, New Jersey and the United Kingdom. There is also the likelihood the perpetra-or made the anthrax himself. He grew it, probably on a solid medium, and weaponised it at a private location where he had accumulated the equipment and the material. We knew that the FBI is looking at this person, and it's likely that he participated in the past in secret activities that the government would not like to see disclosed. And this raises the question of whether the FBI may be dragging its feet some-what and may not be so anxious to bring to public light the person who did this. I knew that they are insiders working for the government, who know this person and who are worried that it could happen that some kind of quiet deal is made that he just disappears from view," said Rosenberg, director of the federations chemical and biological pro-gramme. The FBI declined to comment on the claims.

When I think about these incidents, it makes me wonder what was or was not known with regard to the nineteen hijackers before September 11, 2001. This has subsequently been the subject of inquiry by both the media and Congress. Continued friction between the CIA and the FBI makes us doubt even more.

Because of this information and uncertainty, it is incomprehensible to me why our government does not see or admit the threat that Saudi Arabia poses to America. Barbara Walters, ABC 20/20, had a well documented program on this subject in March 2002 and her observations reflect my own reservations about Saudi Arabia. Reason for concern is evidenced in the following information:

* Fifteen out of the nineteen 9/11 highjackers were from Saudi Arabia. If they had been from Iraq or Iran, I am sure that it would have been reason enough for Washington to declare war on these nations. However, since the Saudi Royal Family donated fifteen million dollars to former President Bush's library as well as other occasional gifts, they are considered our allies and friends.

* Osama bin Laden and many Al-Qaeda leaders are from Saudi Arabia.

*Anti-American propaganda is printed in Saudi government published textbooks and taught in their schools.

* Saudi kings and royal families are incredibly oil rich while the majority of the population lives in poverty.

* Saudi Arabia has been and is a country with strict government rules destined to keep women under the most suppressed conditions; for example, women are forced to wear head to toe cover, "burqas," and not allowed to drive.

* Saudi Arabia donated twenty seven million dollars to Palestinian causes on April 11, 2002 plus an additional one hundred million dollars which was collected in a telethon. One has to wonder if the money was intended for rebuilding demolished Palestinian homes and businesses, and repairing broken water lines or demolished structures from the destruction caused during the Israeli incursion in April and May 2002. Or if much of that large donation was made to

families of suicide bombers, perhaps to recruit more terrorists in Palestine.

* With their wealth and vast territory the Saudis could have proportionally taken in more refugees from the Palestinian camps, just as Jordan, Lebanon, Syria and other neighboring Arab countries did. It would have made this complicated Middle East conflict easier for the rest of the world. But they did not.

As a result of such evidence, I truly am very concerned for the lives and well-being of our troops who are stationed in Saudi Arabia under very precarious and unpredictable conditions.

During President Bush's visit to Pakistan February 13, 2002, CNN had a random street interview with Pakistanis asking their opinion about America's being friends with them. Nine out of ten expressed that "It was not a genuine friendship," because they felt that America's only interest in their country was their need for Pakistan's airspace, bases and support in the war against terrorism in Afghanistan!"

President Bush has been talking about sending troops to Pakistan, Iraq, Georgia, Tajikestan, Azerbaijan, Uzbekistan, the Philippines, Yemen, Iran and other countries in our fight against global terrorism. This could be quite devastating as the conflict in the Middle East itself continues to escalate. Our involvement in too many countries would be spreading ourselves too thin. However, I have this suspicious feeling that the "global war against terrorism" is just a front for us to explore new frontiers for oil.

The American oil companies are the ones who control the pricing of crude oil. It may sound shocking but it is true. They have the power to dictate the price to OPEC (Organization of Petroleum Exporting Countries). For example, in 1998-1999 American oil companies reduced the price so low that OPEC could not produce oil that cheaply. Therefore, some countries purchased oil from us, stored it in their tanks and later sold it at a profit when the price per barrel was raised.

It is hard to believe that we can send a man to the moon, but we seem incapable of finding a viable energy source to replace oil or find ways to use less oil. Can we not produce cars that get more miles per gallon so that we are not dependent on Central Asia's oil for our survival? But in reality, we are not interested in alternative measures, as it seems to many, especially Europeans and Asians, that our master plan is to control the wealth of the world.

Taking into account the extreme poverty and hunger in the Third World nations which produce oil, it would appear that something is deviously and terribly wrong in the distribution of wealth resulting from the oil monies. One would say, how could this possibly be our fault? We do not run their governments, but that's just the point. In many ways our oil companies, foreign policies and leaders do.

We tear the hell out of Afghanistan, dropping bombs worth millions of dollars on a two-dollar piece of dirt, while reporting to the American public that we are rooting out the terrorists. In reality, some critics claim that we are securing ground for a future pipeline from the Caspian Sea. Fox News Channel, in April 2002 interviewed Mr. Gore Vidal, a famous author and historian, who wrote, Perpetual War For Perpetual Peace. Mr. Vidal reinforced my thoughts about the importance of oil in the region to the U.S. Ted Koppel of ABC Nightline also had a two-part program on April 25 and 26, 2002 on this subject. It seems that our politicians and lobbyists make diabolical and incredible deals for the sake of oil and money.

Documents which support what I am writing can be found in the book Bin Laden: The Forbidden Truth by Jean-Charles Brisard and Guillaume Dasquie. Following is a direct quote from the website: http://serendipity.magnet.ch/wot/bl_tft.htm:
"Fact: The World Trade Center (WTC) was bombed
right AFTER Bush-Taliban oil pipe line talks soured. The

98

Talks soured right AFTER Bush/Big Oil threatened Taliban to take their offer or receive a "carpet of bombs." Bush-Cheney/Big Oil and Afghanistan's Taliban negotiated for MONTHS over running a Caspian Sea oil pipeline through Afghanistan. Talks began in February 2001 and continued right on until only one MONTH before New York City's World Trade Center towers were demolished.

DURING the course of these negotiations, the two parties were unable to agree upon a deal, MAINLY because Bush/Big Oil agents constantly upped the ante on the rather naive Taliban representatives: playing intimidation, bait and switch, and "shell" games relentlessly. The Taliban negotiators, understandably, became distrustful of the entire process, and less and less confident they were being dealt with in good faith. In the beginning of August 2001, the Bush Administration and its Big Oil cohorts delivered what amounted to an ultimatum to the Taliban. The Taliban representatives were reportedly told by Bush/Big Oil: Accept our offer of "a carpet of gold or you'll get a carpet of bombs." That's a DIRECT quote, according to French authors Jean-Charles Brisard and Guillaume Dasquie, who've just written a thoroughly-researched and heavily documented book about the entire extraordinary business titled "Bin Laden: The Forbidden Truth." ALSO revealed in the book is the fact that Bush himself directly ordered the FBI and other U.S. law enforcement groups to BACK OFF on TERRORIST-RELATED INVESTIGATIONS while the oil pipeline negotiations were underway! In FACT, The FBI's Deputy Director, John O'Neill resigned in July 2001 in protest over this outrageous and intolerable obstruction. And by the way: the whereabouts of one OSAMA BIN LADEN, then already firmly entrenched at the very top of the US's "most-wanted terrorist" list during the entire course of these pipeline negotiations, was NEVER an issue with the Bush cartel.

Never ONCE were the Taliban urged to hand bin Laden over for all those OTHER horrendous crimes Feds maintain bin Laden has been charged with committing over the years. And so: barely a MONTH after the Bush administration sabotaged the negotiations with the Taliban regarding running the Caspian Sea oil pipeline through Afghanistan, the World Trade Center towers are bombed into oblivion, bringing about the currently ongoing UNDECLARED (and therefore illegal) "war on terrorism"... that just HAPPENS to be directed at the Taliban in Afghanistan.

The WTC was bombed - according to the Feds - by the VERY SAME Osama bin Laden whom the very same Bush administration was so UNCONCERNED ABOUT during those JUST-WRECKED talks with the Taliban. NO ONE but the Bush administration and their Big Oil allies/ accomplices - not the Taliban, not the Palestinians, not ANY other nation whether Islamic or otherwise - not any other group, agency, force or faction on Earth stood to "GAIN" from the destruction of the World Trade Center which occurred only ONE MONTH after talks between the Bush administration "negotiators" and the Taliban fell apart The World Trade Center Demolition and the So-Called War on Terrorism - Serendipity Home Page.

Americans have a difficult time understanding a life of poverty with no hope for basic human rights or relief. Freedom has been given to us at birth; consequently, we have no idea how miserable life is without freedom or hope. Desperation and hopeless situations could quickly turn any pacifist into a warrior.

What happened in Iran under the dictatorship of the late Shah from the 1950's to 1979, and in other countries, for the sake of oil should be considered a good lesson in what not to parrot. However, repeating the same mistakes has been a pattern for our government.

My memories of my life in Iran are still very vivid. His Majesty, the Shah, and his family, plus associates, became richer and richer always paying enough to top American politicians to keep their regime in power. In contrast, the everyday citizen became more miserable, desperate, and poor, so much so that they were prepared to do anything to get rid of the Shah and his government. Ayatollah Khomeini, with the support of the religious militancy, was their only hope to overthrow the Shah and his oppressive dictatorship.

The circumstances are very similar in most Moslem countries today. The vast majority of the population is poor, religious and frustrated. Saudi Arabia, Turkey, Azerbaijan, Turkmenistan, Uzbekistan, Egypt, Tunisia, Tajikestan, Algeria, Jordan, Pakistan, the Philippines, Iraq, and Morocco, to name a few, are prime targets for Islamic fundamentalist takeovers. Iran is held as a model. It's a copy cat situation. Very likely Osama bin Laden or his Al-Qaeda associates would be the leaders in any of those countries with an Islamic takeover. They have been promising the people a much better life by getting rid of the royal families and sharing the country's wealth, which is definitely a clever way to get their support.

Life in Iran is quite similar to that of other neighboring countries in the Middle East. In the Western world people are generally classified socially according to their wealth: the rich, the middle class and the poor. Most Third World countries have their own unique classification. For instance, in my time in Iran, citizens' social categories were:

* The Royal Family and their relatives in a class of their own;
* Beneath the Royal Family, were the upper privileged, and their families, which included prime ministers, cabinet members, government officials, heads of military, secret service, important generals, etc. They were called "The Thousand Families."
* The educated, less than 20% of the citizens, also were the

significant force in the day-to-day operation of the country. This group was comprised of rich, middle class and poor. Doctors, lawyers, judges, educators, officers and business owners were included in this group.

* The vast majority, 80% of the population, fell into the uneducated category. Religion was their inspiration and exclusive way of life. They had two separate classes among them: poor and barely alive. Construction workers, mechanics, blue collar professionals, carpet weavers, and the like were called poor. Four U.S. dollars per day was considered a good income for the highly skilled laborer. Long working hours were part of the trade. Labor was cheap and living expenses were very high. Higher-class citizens employed their maids from this group, who worked for a dollar per day, plus food, housing and clothes.

* The next class, "barely alive," made me wonder how they could survive under such miserable conditions. The absence of water, electricity, food, sanitation and restrooms made it extremely unhealthy. Large families lived in a hole dug in the ground with a bamboo roof.

They called some of those populated areas *Hasir Abad*, meaning the bamboo development. The Shah only featured the glamorous northern section of Tehran as part of his publicity campaign to the world, never showing the unfortunate citizens living in *Hasir Abad* in south Tehran. For most, their only goal in life was to stay alive and survive on that particular day. When I spoke to some, I learned that many didn't know how old they were, what day of the week it was, let alone the year. For most Americans, their pets have a better life!

To further illustrate my point of the discrepancy of wealth and living standards between the East and the West, I have included a chart which lists the Gross Annual National Product Per Capita for some nations. These numbers are taken from Geography, Realms and Regions by deBlij and Muller - 2002.
U.S. = $29,240

Canada = $19,170
Germany = $26,570
Japan = $32,350
Switzerland = $39,980
Pakistan = $470
Tajikistan = $340
Sudan = $290
Iran = $1,650
Nepal = $210
Yemen = $280
India = $440
China = $750

With my close friends in Iran, as part of our civic duty, we delivered bread to some of the poor in hopes of preventing starvation. During our first visits they were so hungry they couldn't wait until we set the bread down. They knocked us to the ground in their frenzy to get a piece. Bread flew everywhere, landing on the dirt road. Even though members of our delivery team were extremely strong athletes, we could not avoid getting injured by the starving villagers. My teammate was a World and Olympic champion wrestler, Golam Reza Takhti. He had three Olympic gold medals along with several world championship and silver medals. This tough man, received serious injuries by taking bread to the poor. Takhti admitted jokingly that no other world wrestler had been able to knock him down as fast as the little starving youngsters did. It became impossible for us to continue our good deed. We had to ask the community leaders to assure our protection before we agreed to go back. I have witnessed children fighting each other over a bone dug out of a trash can, licking it for a little taste of meat.

Meanwhile, the royal families lived in lavish palaces, each constructed for a special season or occasion, each palace more luxurious than the other and in the most beautiful locations on some of the best real estate in the world. These trophy homes were used for gambling, vacations, taking friends, or a mistress, for a weekend of fun. Most would be vacant for years, but the rich had to possess this life style. Ironically, the maids, gardeners, bodyguards and servants were the lucky ones because they were able to enjoy very ritzy surroundings and receive room and board. While at the palace in Iran, the Royal Family's water, fruit, groceries, clothes and all other necessities were flown in daily by private jets. Europe, Japan, Canada and the U.S. were their favorite shopping escapes. Nothing produced locally was good enough for the Royal Family.

As a consequence of these social distinctions, economic sanctions never effect the ruling class, whether in Iran or in other poor countries. Sanctions hurt only the common citizens. Such sanctions also have created economic losses to many American industries by handing a perfect opportunity to other countries, such as Russia, Israel, China, Japan, Germany, and India, to make huge profits.

People like the Shah of Iran, Saddam Hussein of Iraq, Milosevic of Serbia and the late President Deng Xiaoping of China made alliances with any country which served their personal purposes. They didn't "give a hoot" about their own citizens' support or American foreign policies. A government of the people meant nothing to them. The rulers, their top associates, even their employees, had the power to kidnap, rape or kill without the hassle of a legal system interfering. Often citizens' properties and businesses were taken away without recourse. The few who exhibited persistence by making too many inquiries about their possessions mys- teriously disappeared.

During Operation Desert Storm, former President George Bush made a statement: "Our bombing Iraq will put enough pressure on the Iraqi people to realize the need for getting rid of Saddam and replacing him." How bold, as if Mr. Bush didn't know who held the power in that country! Most Americans thought very favorably of the Shah because of his skillful, controlled propaganda. On the contrary, it was all a cover up for what life was really like for the average Iranian! He took basic human rights away from his citizens and made them prisoners in their own country. His two priorities in life were maintaining his power and amassing his own personal wealth. He was a selfish, self-centered man who robbed his own people. With his unlimited wealth stolen from his people, he was able to buy, manipulate and influence American politicians, including our past presidents. I know of no other leader who was capable of being in bed with the Russians and the Americans at the same time. With his exceptional shrewdness and intelligence, he had both the White House and the Kremlin in the palm of his hand, both thinking he was their strongest ally in the Middle East. In the history of modern dictators, the Shah was a true professional at double dealings.

The Shah's enormous wealth, combined with the country's resources and strategic location, made him a very powerful figure. Paying hush money to the international media assured him that his public image would not be tarnished by his orders for mass executions, mutilations and inhumane tortures. Knowing these facts, makes me wonder how our past Presidents could support the late Shah.

The Shah gave the U.S. carte blanche to spy on the Soviet Union. Many Americans think of Iran as being flat, sandy and desert-like. Contrary to this belief, *Alborz,* Iran's highest mountain, has an elevation of 18, 940 ft. It was an ideal location for the U.S. military to install missile surveillance. There they secretly observed and monitored Russian activities. This vantage point was not possible from other neighboring countries because none had as favorable a location. In addition, the Persian Gulf and its oil made Iran an essential and integral Middle Eastern nation for Washington's foreign policy.

The relationship between the Shah and the U.S. was complicated and entwined. The Shah had huge contracts with major American companies, purchasing aircraft, helicopters and weapons. Big businessmen catered to the Shah because he was "big money." They loved the smell of his wealth and opulence. Every mechanical part in Iran, from F-16 bombers to tractors, lawn mowers, electric shavers and calculators, were American-made purchased during the Shah's reign.

The country's survival required American-made parts, a fact which became quite evident during the long eight-year war with Iraq. Replacement parts were needed for every military machine, mostly the fighter bombers. Because of America's economic embargo they were not able to buy them from the United States. Khomeini approached Israel as the middle man in purchasing the parts from the U.S. The shipments were sent to Iran via Switzerland. Russia, China, Japan, Germany, and Switzerland extended their support to the new regime and the flow of needed supplies continued. Indirectly, the Shah's enormous business dealings gave him great power over the lobbyists and politicians on Capitol Hill. Plus, our unconditional support of Israel made some American politicians think that it would be wise if we had Iran on our side, in case the Jewish nation got out of control!

Simultaneously, Iranian natural gas was being piped to Russia - our Evil Empire! It was impossible to conceal the huge pipeline which crossed Iran from the Persian Gulf to Russia. The CIA, U.S. military, and other responsible parties turned a blind eye. The Shah was the kingpin, paying everyone hush money. When people demonstrated for human rights, his Majesty's army would murder the protesters. His army would surround the helpless demonstrators with tanks and helicopters and would then mow them down. In one such mass-killing, which was named Black Friday, his Majesty personally led the helicopters which slaughtered more than 15,000 protesters, mostly women and children. With no respect for the dead and proper burials, bulldozers dumped the bodies into trucks and buried them in mass graves, which is an abomination of Moslem tradition

This entire sordid incident was hidden from the eyes of the world. It wasn't until the overthrow of the Shah that the international news media publicized this horrendous event. How the journalists previously disregarded that awful tragedy was another example of his ability to divert attention from his barbaric criminal acts against the citizens. No one dared to report his horrible crimes against humanity! All Iranians were held hostage by his secret service, SAVAK, trained and supported by the CIA!

The news from Iran was skillfully misleading. I vividly remember a specific campaign the Shah devised, creating much publicity about his granting Iranian women the right to vote. The Americans were very impressed with this show of democracy. However, the voting boxes were fixed by the Shah's men, and he always unanimously won. Is allowing women to go to the polls progress or pure facade? No one in that country had a right to vote, it was only a media show for the West.

Another campaign he promoted was constructing freeways in Tehran. The joke was that the only freeway built was from his palace to his hunting lodge. To add to the injustice, he flew by helicopter to his destinations. This not being public knowledge, the international media again had a field day with headlines boasting of his Majesty's progressive spirit. The Shah never had to deal with the horrendous traffic conditions in Tehran. When he was forced to use ground transportation the entire route would be blocked for several hours before and after his cavalcade. Not even an emergency vehicle was permitted to cross his blockade. He also built a new, fantastic playground in the Persian Gulf called Kiesh Island. It was better than any resort spot in the world. Not for citizens' use, it was his exclusive place of personal enjoyment. This lavish island attracted all the oil rich sheiks in the region to come and spend money in his nightclubs and brothels, which had the most beautiful girls and dancers to serve the wealthy clients.

Briefly, I can describe his Majesty's powerful financial grip in the following manner: whether one takes a cab in Iran or a local flight, stays in a hotel, smokes a cigarette, watches a television show, makes a phone call, buys a Mercedes sedan or a Honda motorcycle, or puts sugar in one's coffee, in each and every case, some of the money landed in a business controlled and owned, in whole or in part, by the Shah or his relatives. Beyond the first family, the Shah's closest friends controlled vast business empires, including monopolies and exclusive concessions conferred by the grace of the Shah. Nepotism, favoritism and corruption have long been ubiquitous. Businesses paid licensing fees off the books. Judges were paid to settle cases. Sweetheart deals were struck between foreign investors and the royal family. Undoubtedly, Iran was one of the most corrupt countries in the world. There was no legitimate legal system; so, one did it their way or paid the consequences.

Regardless of size, businesses in the country were forced to hang a picture of the Shah on the premises. If they did not comply, the business would be closed. Large cash penalties, torture of family members, imprisonment and temporary disappearances of family members were among the customary fines for not having his Majesty's picture hung in a prominent place. Meanwhile, the foreign media misinterpreted this display of photographs as public admiration of the Shah.

The Shah, his family, friends and close associates transferred large sums of money from Iran to foreign bank accounts. Swiss and American banks were among the most popular choices to hide their stolen wealth. He owned much desirable real estate in America and gave numerous holdings to his associates or politicians with whom he dealt. As a result, there are many wealthy Iranians who are living abroad today. Other real estate holdings of the Shah included places in St. Moritz, Panama, Acapulco and Egypt. It is impossible to calculate the amount of money the Royal Family and friends stole from the citizens.

The Iranian National Anthem had nothing to do with Persian history, culture, civilization or the people. It merely said, "Long live the Shah! Because of the Majesty, our land is so wonderful and prosperous." The song continued with further praise of him. The anthem was played over and over, making most Iranians sick to their stomachs. Wherever we went, whatever we did, we had to hear it. Whether in a movie theater, watching a TV program, listening to a lecture, watching sports, or taking a class, one could not escape the lyrics. Everyone was expected to stand up, salute the Shah's image, and then go on with life. If you did not react immediately and with total respect, the SAVAK could arrest you on the spot. There could be many natural little reasons for not responding quickly: if you were in a theater, had an erection because of your sexy date, had a sore back, your clothes got caught in the arm of the chair, it didn't matter, you had to jump up and stand at attention with the first note or else.

Whether one committed a minor or major offense, many never returned from his torture chambers. The Shah had his own sick way of making the punishment fit the crime. There were serious consequences for public wrong doings: blinding people for reading articles against him, so they could never read again; amputating a foot, a leg, or an arm for holding a sign participating in a demonstration for freedom. After the revolution, thousands of people without arms or legs paraded to exhibit the mistreatment they had suffered under the Shah. These amputations were performed in SAVAK torture chambers in Evin Prison in Tehran. The numbers are astonishing, as exemplified by the more than 20,000 mutilated persons participating in some parades.

It is hard to imagine in the history of mankind any other leader as cruel as the Shah. Comparatively speaking there was no other government even under the worst communist rulers which could be compared to the hardships Iranians endured under his regime. One third of Iran's budget was set aside for his secret service, *SAVAK,* operations. During the Nixon administration 3,000 SAVAK members had permission to operate in the U.S. Even in this country, the SAVAK tortured Iranians participating in meetings or activities against the Shah. Bodies were dumped into lakes and ditches; no one the wiser. Hundreds of Iranians living in America were intimidated by a man ruling a country thousands of miles away. How ironic!

The corruption in his government was so appalling that there is no way for me to describe it in a way that most Americans could comprehend. What the police got away with in the police stations was truly a nightmare. Instead of protecting the public, they abused and intimidated the innocent citizens. Each police station had its own team of car thieves and house burglars. They would send the thieves to burglarize homes, returning to the station with the goods, where they were kept in huge storage rooms. Expensive Persian rugs were a hot commodity. The police held the items for two to three months, waiting for the owners to buy back their own goods. If the negotiations were not satisfactory, they would be sold to others. Owners had the chance to buy their own property back, but only for a limited time. The thieves had to provide the police with a detailed list from which house the stolen articles came, plus the date and time they were taken. This enabled the authorities to charge the "proper" fees. If the chief of police or officers wanted an item, they simply took it. No questions asked.

When citizens reported a stolen item, the first question the police asked was, "How much is it worth to you?" Often a similar item from their large storage room was offered when their own stolen property was not available. It was embarrassing to buy something which may have been your neighbor's but who, unfortunately, could not afford the negotiating price with police.

If prostitutes did not pay the police a generous fee and offer their services for free, they could not work the streets.

Often the penalties for not being compliant were severe. Those who did not submit or who were not sexually desirable would be beaten up and their money taken from them. Some became long-term indentured servants. The attractive ones were repeatedly gang raped. The humiliations and constant abuse ensured that everyone complied. Sadly, this practice wasn't limited to hookers. It was common for the Shah's police to extend such vicious abuse to innocent members of any family and their close friends. If for any reason the SAVAK was in search of a person, their family and friends had to pay the price when they could not hand them the suspect or his whereabouts. Imagine being tortured and not having any idea what your crime was!

The Shah employed experienced United States torture experts who worked in Vietnam against the Viet Cong as well as some former CIA torture professionals. They were brought to Iran to train the SAVAK at Evin Prison. They implemented harsh methods such as breaking bones, along with other barbaric torture techniques. Shoving hot, hard-boiled eggs up people's rectums or vaginas to force them to talk was a common practice. If that didn't work, they would hack off an arm or leg of a child, a sister or brother until they received what they wanted.

Without established laws for human rights, there was no way to prove these tortures, let alone stop them. I was struck with the recurring vision of a morning when the entire neighborhood gathered around the smashed body of my neighbor, Hussein, a 59-year-old, well-respected man. His 32-year-old son was part of the underground revolution against the Shah. A team of seven SAVAK members went to his house in search of the son or information leading to his whereabouts. The poor man didn't know how to reach his son as he was an adult and no longer lived at home. Not believing him, they proceeded to tie him up, undressing his wife and four daughters. They brutally gang-raped them one at a time in front of Hussein and the grandchildren to force him to disclose his son's address. The information, he honestly did not have.

The females ranged in age from fourteen to fifty. According to Moslem beliefs, no other man but the husband or immediate family is allowed to see his wife or daughters without the *chador*, or a head scarf, in public. The next day Hussein, unable to deal with his shame, threw himself from the fifth floor of a building. He could not face himself, humiliated and disgraced in front of his family for not being able to protect them. Remembering some of these incidents today still makes me sick to my stomach.

I have a difficult time understanding how America allowed the Shah and his SAVAK to do such inhumane things to his people. It is very hard for me to accept how our intelligence service supposedly missed all of it. I assume money can buy many things, and for the right price many of those responsible parties ignored the principles of freedom and democracy. Former President Carter's motto was "Human Rights," yet he supported the Shah, culminating in the hostage crisis of 1979. I presume Mr. Carter meant human rights for some nations, not the world. President Carter's policies toward Iran were the worst. His actions caused many needless Iranian deaths. In 1980 he ordered all illegal Iranians in the United States to be deported immediately because some Iranians protested against our policies by burning the American flag. His order was illogical. Any person living illegally in a country wouldn't dare to bring attention to themselves in front of international news cameras.

The ones burning the flags were students with legal visas. Iranians living illegally here were low-key, with families and jobs, who stayed out of the limelight. But they were arrested and sent back to Iran. Sadly, in Iran many of those innocent victims were tortured and executed. Khomeini and his associates were suspicious of everyone. It was a critical time trying to hold onto their control. The Iranian officials wrongly labeled the poor returning citizens being sent home from America as part of a CIA spy ring, assigned to overthrow the Ayatollah's new Islamic government.

During the last years of the Shah's reign the U.S. ambassador to Iran was Richard Helms who, before this appointment was the director of the CIA. American politicians and presidents supported the Shah, believing it was necessary to stop the Russians and communism from infiltrating Iran. Communism would have been nothing compared to the dictatorship of the Shah, who in my opinion, was in the same league as Milosevic, Hitler and Saddam. Nothing stopped him from pursuing his cruel criminal actions. The entire nation was held hostage, with every citizen being his victim. By 1979 there was not one family in Iran who did not have at least one member killed, kidnaped, raped or mutilated by his SAVAK. These kinds of actions directly supported by the United States government are impossible for some Moslems to forget today.

Iranians felt they needed a miracle to remove the Shah from power and to kick the US military and CIA out of their country. Much to the Western world's surprise, a man named Ayatollah Khomeini, the most powerful religious leader at the time, was the only person in the world who could overthrow the Shah. Before Khomeini was exiled to France in 1962, he had religious influence over 80 percent of the citizens. The masses flocked to hear his words. This, of course, made the Shah quite nervous. He was not going to let any religious or political leader usurp his hold over the nation. The Shah, who had no problem eliminating anyone, was reluctant to have Khomeini killed because of his tremendous power over the people. Instead he forced Khomeini into exile. The Ayatollah's exile in Paris lasted seventeen years.

Announcing his return to Iran in 1979, through his religious clergymen, the mullahs, he asked the military to put down their weapons and surrender. The Shah's army, with all its strength and power, complied and without bloodshed, the Ayatollah overthrew the Majesty's regime. Iranians poured into the streets, rejoicing in the revolution and Khomeini's homecoming. His loyal followers welcomed him, and the remaining 20% of the population who were not religious, but who could no longer tolerate the Shah, turned to him. He had the entire country behind him. The Shah afraid, seeing the power this man had over the masses, fled the country for the second and the last time.

Unfortunately, the killings and executions resumed after the revolution. This time, however, the ones being executed were the men who had kept the Shah in power. His generals, political leaders and associates posed a threat to Khomeini's takeover, and they had to be eliminated in order to keep the Shah from coming back and regaining his power.

Ayatollah Khomeini was well aware of Iran's history. When Dr. Mohammed Mossaddegh, the country's only hope for freedom and democracy, didn't execute his enemies, he was incarcerated and did not live long enough to see his dreams for a free Iran come true.

The irony was that during Mossaddegh's brief attempt at reforming Iran, his cabinet members, advisors and staff told him to be wary of the Shah's men and the CIA. They knew that the U.S., with the help of some of his generals, was diligently planning to bring the Shah back. All of his associates advised Mossaddegh to either assassinate or incarcerate them. Predating Martin Luther King, Dr. Mossaddegh insisted on nonviolent resistance. He was a supreme human being, believing that murder was inhumane. He wished to establish a true democratic nation, not just a "different" dictatorship.

Twenty-six years later, the Ayatollah Khomeini was not about to make the same mistake. Knowing that the Shah's people could not be trusted, he executed anyone who posed a threat to his newly established Islamic Republic.

Because Khomeini was able to overthrow the Shah easily, the Iranians began to regard him as more than a mere human. As the leader of the new Islamic Republic Government, Khomeini was able to throw the Shah and America out of Iran, and for such was regarded by the majority of the citizens as either a God or his messenger, *Imam*. This spurred a frenzy of religious worship. The United States was caught off guard by his sudden and dramatic takeover. Americans had no time to shut down their military bases, losing billions of dollars in military equipment. All our soldiers and the civilians were evacuated leaving everything behind, just as occurred in Vietnam years later.

The year 1981 was the first time in history Iranians were given the right to choose their own president. Again, in May 1997 they went to the polls and elected an educated, moderate president, Mr. Khatami, and they reelected him in 2001. Life for Iranians is slowly starting to make some progress. I am hoping and praying that they will finally have some happiness, basic human rights and freedom which they so deserve. I also hope that our government will not interfere and overthrow their leadership with another military coup. The right thing to do would be to extend a hand to establish diplomacy, social and economic trade between the two nations. This would be a step in the right direction in helping establish a democratic society for the Iranian people. Regrettably, Washington instead for the third time vetoed Iran's membership in the World Trade Community in the United Nations.

Since 1980 Iranian assets in the United States have been frozen. President Khatami's interview with Christiane Amanpour on January 7, 1998 on CNN titled "Iran - A New Beginning" indicated how ready and willing Iran is to put the past behind and start a new, healthy diplomatic relationship with the United States. He asked for an exchange of ideas and invited Americans to come to Iran. The American government did little or nothing to open communication between Tehran and Washington, and instead four years later, insultingly, has labeled Iran as part of the "Axis of Evil." Such diplomatic blindness hurts me to my very core.

For decades Russians and Chinese were thought of as our enemies. Now they are considered as "friends." Ironically, however, the Russian Mafia operates in the United States as one of the most dangerous of terrorist groups.

Thrown back to the Dark Ages by the Islamic Republic, strapped by a poor economy, with power outages, water shortages, and food lines as routine occurrences, the country is bankrupt. Lack of medication and the necessities of life have created terrible living conditions. Today, Iran is rife with problems.

It would not be out of line to say that there might be another American coup trying to bring Reza Pahlavi to power in Iran. I hope my prediction is wrong. Barbara Walters in February 2002 -20/20, interviewed Reza Pahlavi, who claimed that the Iranian people want him to return to Iran to replace the Islamic Republic. I suspect that Mr. Pahlavi, who was one of the benefactors in his father's fortune, is continuing in his father's footsteps. Thinking of it made me angry because Khatami is the elected leader, no matter what we think. President George W. Bush has been referring to Iran as part of the Axis of Evil and hinting at Iran's need for a change in regime. In any case, I would not be surprised to learn that Mr. Pahlavi is one of the advisors to the White House regarding policies made about Iran.

8 - THE FINAL POINT

Moslems have a well-known, common proverb: "A friend of my enemy is my enemy and the pain of my friend hurts me also." In the Middle East people mourn for the suffering of all the dead, mutilated or starving children of fellow Moslems. The concern and compassion is heard in their daily prayers in which they ask Allah's mercy for the victims and their families.

Professor Houston Smith believes: "Terrorists are not savages who can be calmed only by occupation." The solution ironically can be found in the prophets of Israel. As Isaiah saw it, it is only if you plant justice that you will have peace (Isa. 32). Occupation of another people's land is not justice nor is taking the livelihood away from starving, innocent people.

It is time for Americans to understand and be sure that our policies are not based on hurting the general population of these countries in conflict. Wherever we practice duplicity, we will be paid in the same manner. We cannot condone terror in one place, then condemn and complain about it in another. Terror or killing is unacceptable, regardless of who is doing it or for whatever the reasons given.

It is my sincere hope and wish that we stay away from "covert operations and interfering in the internal affairs of other nations." If some countries want to destroy themselves or each other, it is sad but we must let them determine their own destiny without getting ourselves caught in their line of fire.

Middle Easterners have a different mentality, difficult for Westerners to understand. I do not mean that they are "right or wrong," but merely that they are different and must be dealt with accordingly. They hate America because of our policies toward them; they are not against our democracy and freedom, which many of our politicians claim time after time. Their reactions are not based on our system of government, as they would do the same if America were a dictatorship or socialist.

The unpredictable history of the Middle East is reflected in

117

the following well-known fable which captures the complex essence of their politics and cultural thought:

A scorpion came out of the Sahara desert to the banks of the Nile, where he approached a crocodile. "My dear friend," he said to the crocodile, "could we form an alliance to get to the other side of the Nile?"

The crocodile answered, "What do you think, I am stupid? Why should I put myself at your complete mercy? You could sting me and kill me at any time during our crossing."

"Why would you even think that?" said the scorpion. "Trust me; you are safe with me. If I sting you, then I will drown."

Thinking this over the crocodile agreed that the scorpion made sense, so he took the scorpion on his back. In the middle of the stream the scorpion, agitated because the crocodile was swimming slowly, stung the crocodile.

As the two were about to go under, the crocodile turned to the scorpion and said, "Now we both will die. What possible logic is there for such a behavior?"

"There is none" replied the scorpion, *this is the Middle East*!

In addition, a basic law of physics dictates that "For every action there is an equal and opposite reaction." America has been fortunate that other countries where we have committed injustice have not retaliated or attacked us prior to the 9/11 incident.

President Bush said: "We should have been taking care of Saddam Hussein in Iraq when we had the chance by finishing the job. All American politicians along with the majority of our citizens agree with him. But not many people ask: "Then what?" Is taking Saddam out of power going to assure us of peace in the Middle East or put an end to all our problems? Definitely not. There would be another trouble maker in his place, perhaps Reza, Abdullah, Mohammed or Omar. In the larger, long-term picture, Saddam is an insignificant pawn. We have more serious global issues to deal with than taking care of one man. It seems that President Bush has a personal vendetta because of what happened with his father when Saddam was a party to a failed assassination plot to former President Bush.

Most recent evidence of our dubious position in the eyes of the world is seen in Dick Cheney's mission to the Middle East and Europe in April 2002. Mr. Cheney tried to gain support for a possible attack on Iraq but his efforts were a total failure. Not one out of eleven countries he visited showed the slightest interest to go along with President Bush's plan.

It was not surprising to see that the President's visit to Germany on May 22, 2002 in trying to personally gain support for an attack against Iraq ended up in another failure when more than 20,000 German protesters expressed their opposition to Mr. Bush's plans for a military fight against terrorism. The following news from MSNBC on that day is proof of many Europeans' feelings about American policies:

"THOUSANDS of protesters massed the day before to oppose any widening of the anti-terrorism campaign as Bush began his first visit to Germany. Police estimated that 20,000 demonstrators gathered near his hotel. And while the protests were mostly peaceful, violence broke out among groups of hooded youths and pro-Palestinian demonstrators. An American flag was burned, and demonstrators pelted police in riot gear with bottles and stones. Officials said 44 people were injured and some 50 demonstrators detained. The protesters were kept far away from Bush and his entourage by multiple barricades and some 10,000 police officers, the largest police operation in Berlin since World War II! More protests on issues ranging from Iraq to the environment and trade were planned in the city later on Thursday and security remained high. Bush is under fire in Europe - over what many view as U.S. uni- lateralism concerning key questions such as global warming, international justice and trade."

Demonstrations were also held in France and Italy.

If we are so concerned with Iraq's "nuclear power" for mass destruction, why don't we Americans go after the source to stop such dangerous resources from reaching Saddam's hands? Why is it that "friendly countries" selling him nuclear materials is not a big deal but his buying them is? We conveniently turn a blind eye to the fact that China, Russia, France and other countries are selling him these materials. We excuse our inconsistency by saying those countries are our friends. This is an excellent example of double standards by our politicians.

I am not implying that we should let Saddam or anyone else destroy other countries with nuclear weapons or even possess them. But we must be consistent in our standards, actions and policies, including "friendly" countries like India and Pakistan. In spite of President Bush's accusations, it should be noted, however, that Mr. Scott Ritter, a UNSCOM inspector reporting in an MSNBC interview on May 3, 2002, testified that Iraq has NO capability to make "weapons of mass destruction."

We should take note that Europe, Canada, Australia and New Zealand have had little if any threat with terrorist attacks because they leave other countries alone. I admire Europe for the way they have recovered from the near-total destruction by two World Wars. Looking at Japan and how they have rebuilt their country after the devastation of the atomic bomb makes us realize that the event of 9/11 was minuscule compared to what they had to cope with. Of course they could not have done so well without American help, but their recovery has been astonishing.

All terrorism is inhuman and tragic! The anthrax threat, the blowing up of a government building in Oklahoma, the Columbine school shooting, the Palestinian suicide bombers, the Israeli incursion with mass murders, and we must not forget the horror of the Irish Protestant/Catholic conflict, all have torn

120

my heart. I ran away from a harsh dictatorship and a hardline, religious government in pursuit of "freedom." I have been very fortunate to find my dream in America and I will not allow anyone to "take my hard-earned liberty away from me." I pray that all the other Americans will feel the same so that together we can appreciate what we have and who we are and not casually take innocent lives in countries where we do not belong.

The poor of the world see us and evaluate us with an absence of pity. As many as one billion people in the world live in absolute poverty; 79% of them are women and children. Forty million people die each year from hunger and hunger-related causes. Poverty kills. This is the equivalent of 320 jumbo jet planes crashing every day with the majority of the passengers being children (A Green History of the World by Clive Ponting). This said, the combination of hunger and discontent requires us to display compassion and humane efforts and NOT rely on war if we desire to have peace.

Gerd Theissen, the biblical scholar, noted the century long quest for the missing link between apes and "true" humanity. "Call off the search," he said. "The missing link is us. True humanity could not do what we have done to one another and to this generous host of the earth."

Karen Armstrong, the author of The Battle for God: A History of Fundamentalism and Islam: A Brief History, wrote an article, *Ghosts of our Past* for Modern Maturity magazine, February 2002 which I strongly recommend. Her thinking is parallel to mine, "to win the war against terrorism, we first need to understand its roots." Ms. Armstrong concludes her article with:

> "We in the First World must develop a *one world* mental-ity in the years to come. We cannot leave the fight against terrorism solely to our politicians or to our armies.
> Ordinary citizens must find out more about the rest of the

world. We must find out about foreign ideologies and other religions like Islam. And we must also acquire a full knowledge of our own governments' foreign policies, using our democratic rights to oppose them, should we deem this necessary."

The Peace Corps, since 1961, has provided volunteer skilled teachers, builders, counselors etc. who have assisted people of underdeveloped nations. This has been a fantastic service! They have proven what "true" humanity is all about. It is a worthy cause to promote the welfare of mankind and the best way to show American character and kindness. The legacy that the American Peace Corps has left by educating and demonstrating how to be more productive wherever they went is a much better representation of our country than all our bombings.

We must now look much beyond America's isolated shores and deep into the eyes of the world. I am proud to say that if there is a nation on earth having that capability it is the United States. We have the capacity for reflection, understanding, wisdom and fairness which are the prerequisites for peace on Earth. We can lead and lead well. Let us not squander this great opportunity. Let us show the world that Americans are the symbols of truth, humanity and decency, not just self-seeking capitalists.

In conclusion these are my global wishes, for all humankind: *Inshallah!*

Where there is pain, I wish for *peace and mercy.* Where there is doubt, I wish for the *ability to work through it.* Where there is tragedy, hurt or sadness, I wish for *patience, forgiveness and renewed strength.* Where there is hate I wish for *love, courage and understanding.*

APPENDIX

About the Author: Firooz E. Zadeh is a very proud American by choice since 1980. He was born into a wealthy Iranian family in 1938 and raised a Moslem in the Middle East. He was denied food, clothing and affection by his abusive father, a careless mother and a mean stepmother. His early life was one of constant struggle. Deprivation, starvation and physical abuse are his unhappy childhood memories.

He was raised by his paternal stepmother, an exceptional human being, Tala who taught him how to ignore the physical pain and reach for the highest possible goal. The conditions along with Tala's teachings made him learn at an early age to depend upon himself and his own resources.

The first 12 years of his schooling in Iran included compulsory Islamic studies. In 1967 because of his athletic talent as a former Iranian national athlete he was hired to coach soccer at the University of Wyoming.

He has a B.S. from the University of Tehran, a M.S. from the University of Wyoming and his doctoral studies were at the University of Northern Colorado and Denver University. He retired as the most outstanding teacher in 1995 from Eagle County School District, in Colorado and taught Geography at Colorado Mountain College.

His lectures about Islam, the Middle East, learning English in America, cultural differences, and global understanding are among the most popular presentations on cruise lines.

Firooz's unique talent to inspire others, especially young adults, to perform their best, to go for the gold is a rare quality. He knows how to instill confidence, self-worth and hope in others, by believing *the impossible just takes a little longer.*

Barbara Clary, a parent, expressing sadness at his retirement stated: "Whatever Firooz chooses to do next, his involvement will make a difference in someone's life."

57 Member of the OIC and the year they joined and 3 Observer States.

Afghanistan   1969
Albania, Republic of   1992
Algeria, People's Democratic Republic of   1969
Azerbaijan, Republic of   1991
Bahrain, State of   1970
Bangladesh, People's Republic of   1974
Benin, Republic of   1982
Brunei Dar-us-Salaam, Sultanate of   1984
Burkina Faso   1975
Cameroon, Republic of   1975
Chad, Republic of   1969
Comoros, Federal Islamic Republic of the   1976
Cote d'Ivoire, Republic of   2001
Djibouti, Republic of 1978
Egypt, Arab Republic of   1969
Gabon, Republic of   1974
Gambia, Republic of the   1974
Guinea, Republic of   1969
Guinea-Bissau, Republic of   1974
Guyana, Republic of   1998
Indonesia, Republic of   1969
Iran, Islamic Republic of   1969
Iraq, Republic of   1976
Jordan, Hashemite Kingdom of   1969
Kazakhstan, Republic of   1995
Kuwait, State of   1969
Kyrghyzistan, Republic of   1992
Lebanon, Republic of 1969
Libya, Socialist People's Libyan Arab Jamahiriya   1969
Malaysia   1969
Maldives, Republic of   1976
Mali, Republic of   1969

Mauritania, Islamic Republic of   1969
Morocco, Kingdom of   1969
Mozambique, Republic of   1994
Niger, Republic of   1969
Nigeria, Federal Republic of   1986
Oman, Sultanate of   1970
Pakistan, Islamic Republic of 1969
Palestine, State of   1969
Qatar, State of   1970
Saudi Arabia, Kingdom of   1969
Senegal, Republic of   1969
Sierra Leone, Republic of   1972
Somalia, Democratic Republic of   1969
Sudan, Republic of the   1969
Surinam, Republic of the   1996
Syrian Arab Republic 1970
Tajikistan, Republic of   1992
Togo, Republic of   1997
Tunisia, Republic of   1969
Turkey, Republic of   1969
Turkmenistan, Republic of   1992
Uganda, Republic of   1974
United Arab Emirates, State of   1970
Uzbekistan, Republic of   1995
Yemen, Republic of   1969

* * * * *

A review of
Bin Laden: The Forbidden Truth
by Jean-Charles Brisard and Guillaume Dasquie
French authors Jean-Charles Brisard and Guillaume Dasquie
recently published a book entitled Bin Laden: The Forbidden
Truth which tells of the negotiations for oil pipeline rights in
Afghanistan that collapsed in August 2001 after the U.S. told

the Taliban: Accept our offer of a carpet of gold or you'll get a carpet of bombs.

U.S. Policy on Taliban Influenced by Oil
By Julio Godoy

Under the influence of United States oil companies, the government of President George W. Bush initially blocked intelligence agencies' investigations on terrorism while it bargained with the Taliban on the delivery of Osama bin Laden in exchange for political recognition and economic aid, two French intelligence analysts claim.

In the book, "Bin Laden, La Verite Interdite" (Bin Laden, the Forbidden Truth), that was released recently, the authors, Jean-Charles Brisard and Guillaume Dasquie, reveal that the Federal Bureau of Investigation's (FBI) Deputy Director John O'Neill resigned in July in protect in protest over obstruction.

The authors claim that 'O'Neill told them that "the main obstacles to investigate Islamic terrorism were U.S. oil corporate interests and the role played by Saudi Arabia in it. "The two claim that the U.S. government's main objective in Afghanistan was to consolidate the position of the Taliban regime to obtain access to the oil and gas reserves in Central Asia.

They affirm that until August 2001, the U.S. government saw the Taliban regime" as a source of stability in Central Asia that would enable the construction of an oil pipeline across Central Asia" from the rich oilfields in Turkmenistan, Uzbekistan and Kazakhstan, through Afghanistan and Pakistan, to the Indian Ocean. Until now, says the book. " the oil and gas reserves of Central Asia have been controlled by Russia. the Bush government wanted to change all that." But, confronted with Taliban's refusal to accept U.S. conditions, "this rationale of energy security changed into a military one," the authors claim.

"At one moment during the negotiations, the U.S. representatives told the Taliban, 'either you accept our offer of a carpet of gold, or we bury you under a carpet of bombs," Brisard said in an interview in Paris. (This threat was made *before* September 11th.)

According to the book, the Bush Administration began to negotiate with the Taliban immediately after coming into power in February. U.S. and Taliban diplomatic representatives met several times in Washington, Berlin, Islamabad.

To polish their image in the United States, the Taliban even employed a U.S. expert on public relations, Laila Helms. The authors claim that Helms is also an expert in the works of U.S. intelligence organizations, for her uncle, Richard Helms, is a former Director of the Central Intelligence Agency (CIA).

The last meeting between U.S. and Taliban representatives took place in August, five weeks before the attacks on New York and Washington, the analysts maintain. On that occasion, Christina Rocca, in charge of Central Asian affairs for the U.S. government, met the Taliban Ambassador to Pakistan (Abdul Salam Zaeef) in Islamabad.

Brisard and Dasquie have long experience in intelligence analysis. Brisard was until the late 1990s Director of economic analysis and strategy for Vivendi, a French company. He also worked for French secret services, and wrote for them in 1997 a report on the now famous Al-Qaeda network, headed by bin Laden.

Dasquie is an investigative journalist and publisher of Intelligence Online, a respected newsletter on diplomacy, economic analysis and strategy, available through the Internet.

Brisard and Dasquie draw a portrait of the closest aides to Bush, linking them to oil business. Bush's family has a strong oil background, as do some of his top aides. From Vice President Dick Cheney, through the Director of the National Security Council Condoleezza Rice, to the secretaries of commerce and energy, Donald Evans and Stanley Abraham, all have long worked for U.S. oil companies.

Cheney was until the end of last year President of Halliburton, a company that provides services for oil industry; Rice was between 1991 and 2000 manager for Chevron; Evans and Abraham worked for Tom Brown, another oil giant.

Besides the secret negotiations held between Washington and Kabul and the importance of the oil industry, the book takes issue with the role played by Saudi Arabia in fostering Islamic fundamentalism, in the personality of bin Laden, and with the networks that the Saudi dissident built to finance his activities.

Brisard and Dasquie contend that the U.S. government's claim that it had been prosecuting bin Laden since 1998 (is a big fraud). "Actually," Dasquie says, "the first state to officially prosecute bin Laden was Libya, on charges of terrorism."

"Bin Laden wanted to settle in Libya in the early 1990s, but was hindered by the government of Muammar Gaddafi," Dasquie claims. "Enraged by Libya's refusal, bin Laden organized attacks inside Libya, including assassination attempts against Gaddafi."

Dasquie singles out one group, the Islamic Fighting Group (IFG), reputedly the most powerful Libyan dissident organization, based in London, and directly linked with bin Laden. "Gaddafi even demanded Western police institutions, such as Interpol, to pursue the IFG and bin Laden, but never obtained cooperation," Dasquie says. "Until today, members of IFG openly live in London".

The book confirms earlier reports that the U.S. government worked closely with the United Nations during the negotiations with the Taliban. "Several meetings took place this year, under the arbitration of Frances Vendrell, personal representative of UN secretary-general Kofi Annan, to discuss the situation in Afghanistan," says the book. "Representatives of the U.S. government and Russia, and the six countries that border with Afghanistan were present at these meetings," it says. "Sometimes, representatives of the Taliban also sat around the table."

These meetings, also called Six plus Two, because of the number of states (six neighbors plus the U.S. and Russia) involved, have been confirmed by Niaz A. Naik, former Pakistani Secretary for foreign affairs.

In French television news program two weeks ago, Naik said that during a Six plus Two meeting in Berlin in July, the discussions turned around "the formation of a government of national unity. If the Taliban had accepted this coalition, they would have immediately received international economic aid. And the pipelines from Kazakhstan and Uzbekistan would have come," he added.

Naik also claimed that Tom Simons, the U.S. representative at these meetings, openly threatened the Taliban and Pakistan. Simons said: "either the Taliban behave as they ought to, or Pakistan convinces them to do so, or we will use another option". The words Simons used were a "military operation," Naik claimed.   (Asia Times Online)

* * * * *

Iranian Abandons Push To Improve U.S. Ties
The Washington Post - Thursday, May 30, 2002

TEHRAN, May 29 -- President Mohammad Khatami urged his reformist allies in parliament today to abandon a quest for better relations with the United States because of what he described as the growing U.S. belligerence toward Iran.

Khatami, a moderate cleric who made a dramatic overture to the United States in 1997, said he was put off by the tone U.S. leaders have taken toward Iran.

"When a big power uses a militant, humiliating and threatening tone to speak to us, our nation will refuse to negotiate or show any flexibility," he said at a meeting with members of parliament, where his allies hold a majority.

He called on supporters to abandon efforts to reach out to

the United States and said they should follow Iran's official policy instead. Defying old taboos on relations with Washington, reformist lawmakers have held closed-door meetings to explore ways of resolving two decades of hostilities between the two countries.

The move drew rebukes from Iran's supreme religious leader, Ayatollah Ali Khamenei, and threats by the hard-line judiciary to prosecute anyone who advocated dialogue with "the Great Satan." And a hard-line lawmaker today accused those favoring ties of being U.S. spies.

Iran's Supreme National Security Council, headed by Khatami, has reportedly ruled out talks with Washington in reaction to charges by President Bush that Iran is part of an "axis of evil" with Iraq and North Korea.

* * * * *

Longmont Daily Times-Call
April 24, 2002
"Hundreds of Airport Workers Arrested on Fraud"
Under the governments zero tolerance policy in its war on terrorism, Federal officials expected to arrest 138 employees at Dulles International Airport and Ronald Reagan Washington International Airport on charges that they lied about previous criminal connections, used false social security numbers or were in the country illegally.

An additional ten workers were arrested at Baltimore Washington International Airport, the U.S. Attorney's office in Baltimore said.

Since the September 11 terrorist attacks, 450 employees at 14 airports have been indicted or arrested, officials said.
The Associated Press

* * * * *

On Bush's trip, discordant messages
President's reputation as bumbler revived in Europe
Mike Allen and Dana Milbank - *THE WASHINGTON POST*

May 30, 2002 - After a church service during President Bush's week-long European tour, French President Jacques Chirac surprised Bush, who had not planned to speak, by leading him to a stage and delivering a long speech that included criticism of U.S. policies.

* * * * *

Karen Armstrong, the author of The Battle for God:
A History of Fundamentalism and Islam: A Brief History
"Throughout the Muslim world there is widespread bitterness against America, even among pragmatic and well-educated businessmen and professionals, who may sincerely deplore the recent atrocities (September 11), condemn them as evil, and feel sympathy with the victims, but who still resent the way the Western powers have behaved in their countries. This atmosphere is highly conducive to extremism, especially now that potential terrorists have seen the catastrophe that it is possible to inflict using only the simplest of weapons.

Even if President Bush and our allies succeed in eliminating Osama bin Laden and his network, hundreds more terrorists will rise up to take their place unless we in the West address the root cause of this hated. This task must be an essential part of the war against terrorism."

BIBLIOGRAPHY

Qur'an - Koran

The Battle for God: A History of Fundamentalism *and* Islam: A Brief History - Karen Armstrong

Marie Claire magazine - Jan Goodwin - April 2002

ABC news.com: May 17, 2002 - May 23, 2002

Organization of Islamic Conference (IOC) Website and Press Release: (19 Feb. 2001 -

25 July 2001- 12 Sept. 2001 - 1 Oct. 2001)

Nine Parts of Desire - The Hidden World of Islam Women - Geraldine Brooks

"Genesis of International Terrorism" - Dr. Eqbal Ahmed

The New York Times - Dec. 18, 1985

Fighting Terrorism - Benjamin Netanyahu

"Cycle of Violence" - MSNBC - March 7, 2002

As-Safir Newspaper - Hisham Melhem - March 7, 2002

Nightline - Ted Koppel - special programs (1980 - 2002)

See No Evil - Robert Baer

A Bird of Passage - Otto Lang

Middle East Conflict - Mitchell Bard

2000 WorldNetDaily.com - Joseph Farah

Webster's New World Dictionary, Third College Edition

Geography, Realms, Regions and Concepts 2002 - H.J. de Blij and Peter O. Muller

MSNBC - Brian Williams - Feb. 27, 2002

Lonely Planet - China 5th Edition

In Retrospect - The Tragedy and Lessons of Vietnam - Robert McNamara

War Remnants Museum brochure - Ho Chi Minh City, Vietnam

Time Magazine - Michael Elliott - March 11, 2002

People Magazine - Peter Noram and Eileen Finan - April 12, 2002

New Zealand Herald - Rupert Cornwall - Feb. 21, 2002
New Zealand Herald - Andrew Buncombe - Feb. 21, 2002
Perpetual War For Perpetual Peace - Gore Vidal
Bin Laden: The Forbidden Truth - Jean-Charles Brisard and Guillaume Dasquie
A Green History of the World - Clive Ponting
Internet: Yahoo Education Reference: Factbook
MSNBC.com
ABC.com - Nightline - 20/20
CBS - 60 Minutes
NBC Meet the Press - Tim Russert
Jihad in America - Steve Anderson
E-mails and additional information from Masood Ahmad
Television Broadcasts in Europe, Asia and New Zealand
The Denver Post - International Affairs - "Couple Endure Cultural Clashes"
The Washington Post - "Iranian Abandons Push to Improve U.S. Ties - May 30 ,2002
Eric Margolis - Foreign Affairs Writer
Poverty from the Wealth of Nations - Shahdid Alam
TOP VIEW - New Book (Bin Laden: The Forbidden Truth) Details Bush/Big Oil Negotiations With Taliban Before WTC
Lara Marlowe: U.S. Efforts to Make Peace Summed up by 'Oil'
ABC News. com - FBI Was Warned of Sept. 11 Hijacker- "Informant Says He Provided Facts About Phoenix Hijacker" May 23, 2002

The late Shah of Iran admiring my National Championship
medal at an international Boy Scout Leadership camp, 1960.